YOU ARE NOT WHO YOU THINK YOU ARE!

Phil Hughes

To my beloved brother David.

This book is dedicated to you and your beautiful memory.

In every heartbeat, breath and step we take,

In the words we speak

You are here.

"There is nothing outside which can help you, there is nothing outside which can hurt you, because there is no outside."

Sydney Banks

"Truth can never change its nature, whereas untruth is always changing."

Tripura Rahaysa

"Let what comes come; let what goes go. Find out what remains."

Ramana Maharshi

x

"I am that by which I know "I am.""

Nisargadatta Maharaj

CONTENTS

FOREWORD

.

The foreword to a book is generally that annoying part at the start that most just cursorily thumb through and move on.

That redundant couple of pages inside the front cover - after the moderately helpful Contents page - that the fastidious must churn through in order to maintain their "cover to cover" credentials, while most frustratedly brush past in order to get to The Action.

In short, no one really reads it. Other than as a courtesy. Or a compulsion.

On a much rarer occasion, a foreword shows up a qualitatively different beast; something truly worthy of the name.

A gentle "on ramp" to what is to follow. Wise, insightful, helpful even. Hinting, introducing, alluding. A promise of what is to come; but without in any way giving the game away such that it spoils things or renders ongoing endeavours nugatory.

It is with the distinct pleasure of attempting to produce something worthy of the genre that I have on this occasion been tasked.

Having been given the opportunity to follow the production of the work that you now hold in your hands as it has evolved and taken shape over the preceding months, my hope is that my endeavours will do justice to what I know is to follow.

I met Phil a little upwards of six years ago, on a course we were both attending. He as a participant. I in a supporting role. I liked him instantly.

For as those of you reading this who have had the pleasure of making his acquaintance will likely attest, he is one of those instantly likeable souls. One from whom – in his own quiet but assured way - goodness and gentle humility radiate.

As it does from each and every page of his work.

I hope that those of you who have not met him may some day get this chance. Those who may not do so in person, will get the opportunity to come closer to this in the following pages.

Second only perhaps to inapposite book forewords in the canon of modern day redundancies is perhaps books themselves. And that coming from a self-professed bibliophile.

With the advent of technological advances and the increasing automation of the affairs of the world, publishing has become less the esoteric art form; such that it is now readily accessible to many more people.

As with most technological changes, advancement has proven the proverbial double-edged sword.

Increased accessibility has bought with it the opportunity for just about anyone to become a published author. Allied with even a minimal degree of adeptness in creating a social media following, fabled "best seller" status often follows closely behind.

In short, a great many books now written and published are – in my perhaps not so humble opinion – not necessarily so worthy of being so. The world would not miss out one iota were they not.

Extravagant business and calling cards, rather than genuine efforts to codify the individual and collective wisdom in service of helping the world spin a little smoother on its energetic axis.

So it is rare in this day and age - and ironically more so in the so-called Personal Development space - to find a book that is truly written for the right reasons. One that offers something different. Something worthy of its pages, its ink, its binding and its readership.

Phil Hughes is one of the few who bucks the trend.

In the pages that follow, he will take you on a journey. Not by force, or by persuasion. But by gentle, graceful, invitation.

As all the best ones are. And in the only way he could.

You will meet Phil. The man. The human being. The beautiful soul I alluded to above. And you will have the opportunity to take a front row seat for some of the more formative, poignant and noteworthy moments of his life.

Beyond this, and behind the personal narrative, you will be offered a glimpse, a channel, a portal - to a deeper understanding of what it means to be a human on Planet Earth.

An exploration and exposition of the workings and machinations of the human mind. The human spirit. And the human soul.

What this will do for you remains to be told. But I counsel you in the strongest possible terms to be willing to make the voyage with him and see for yourself.

There is no need to analyse or cogitate as you do this. Or to think too much about what you are offered. For I offer that the part of you that stands to gain from what he shares is not the part that could do that even if it tried.

This is deeper than that. And any effort you could apply to this end, will likely defeat itself.

So relax, and enjoy the journey.

There's nothing to get that you don't have. Other than a deeper appreciation of what you undoubtedly already do.

On that note, and with all my love, I will leave you in Phil's incredibly capable hands. And allow him to point the way.

Jonny Bowden
Wiltshire, Feb 2021

INTRODUCTION

Once upon a time there was a boy named Phil.

To begin with of course, Phil did not know this.

The world was simply a collection of indistinct shapes and sensations.

Over time, Phil became aware that there were things he apparently controlled and was able to move by himself.

He didn't know these things were called fingers and toes, but he did once he began to learn words.

He became aware that the world was split into a me and a not me.

The me seemed to be contained by the body.

The not me was everything else.

The not me was quite scary, as it was a lot bigger than the me.

But there were two not me's who seemed to care very much for him, and they were around most of the time - they fed him, cleaned him and made him feel better when he got upset.

They also taught him his name was Phil, although where they got that information from, he had no idea.

He simply took it on faith. The two not me's - his parents - seemed to know everything, so why wouldn't he trust them?

He began to learn about who Phil was.

Phil was apparently a bit sickly and suffered from a breathing condition called asthma.

Because his left hand didn't work very well a doctor set it in a splint to correct it, but it didn't help, and the hand hung at an awkward angle that other people's hands didn't.

Then Phil fell off a table and twisted his Achilles heel, which impaired the growth and flexibility of his left leg.

Others suggested that these conditions put limits on what he could achieve.

He got teased at school because of the hand, and the way his mother coddled him.

He loved football, but football didn't love him. He was usually the last to be picked, and he wondered if it was because of the hand or the leg.

He gravitated towards individual sports like badminton and golf.

Golf was his mother and father's chosen sport, which meant he could spend time with them doing something they all loved.

It was fun, and he got quite good at it despite his limitations.

When he started competing, he would get angry when he hit a golf shot that was less than perfect. He knew he was capable of better, why couldn't he produce it at will, every time?

His mother and father would get embarrassed when he had a temper tantrum on the course.

It was not the way to behave, he was showing them up, and he mustn't be that way.

But Phil wanted to be perfect at something, and so he continued working to improve and the tantrums kept happening.

Golf became a barometer of his self-worth - if he played well, he was worth something, but if he didn't, he was useless. His moods were likewise calibrated - the world was either wonderful or miserable according to how golf went.

When Phil was fifteen, his dad left his mum. His mum was devastated. She believed she could not start again at her time of life. Two bad marriages and she decided she was not meant to find true love. That was the way of it.

Together with his beloved older brother, Phil became her prop, listening to hours of her rehashing the past twenty-three years, wondering where it had gone wrong.

Phil didn't have too much time to think about himself - he was too involved helping mum - but when he did have a moment, he wondered if he were the cause.

His dad had been his idol, and that idol now lay shattered in pieces.

He heard the whispers at school. The other kids knew. They were talking about him, and now it wasn't just about the hand.

He developed quite spectacular acne.

At its apogee, his cheeks resembled the sides of Vesuvius.

There were girls he liked at school, but he dare not talk to them. He'd felt the pain of rejection once too often and didn't want to experience it again.

University did him the world of good. It taught him that he could look after himself.

He also made lots of friends who accepted him for who he was and didn't tease him about his shortcomings.

Many of his friends were girls. They seemed to like him because of his empathetic side that one friend said he must have developed when helping his mother through the separation.

That empathy seemed to doom him to be seen as friend material though, and not boyfriend material.

That was the way it appeared to him. In any case, he didn't know how to go about developing THAT kind of relationship. He didn't have the confidence.

He did have a growing belief in his ability to live independently though, fostered by university and two summers living and working in Germany.

His childhood town of Great Yarmouth had seemed like the entire world, but after university and two summers in Munich speaking German with the locals, the world had gotten much bigger.

He could see how much there was to be explored.

He went travelling in America with one of his closest friends.

The American cities were alive, vibrant, exciting.

Great Yarmouth now seemed such a quiet, isolated backwater by comparison.

Phil wanted something like the American experience when he returned home.

There was only one place he could think of which was comparable, and so, like, Dick Whittington, he went off to London. Minus the cat.

Although he had a limited number of friends, he instantly loved it, and after a couple of false starts landed a great job at a big multi-national.

He found he could make people laugh quite easily, so used that to get closer to people.

He gradually widened his circle of friends, and life was good.

But he still wanted to be happier. To be better at work, on the golf course and in daily life.

He wanted to find love. He still possessed an unerring ability to convert romantic possibilities into friendships.

He still wasn't confident that he was worthy of love.

He began reading golf psychology, positive psychology and spiritual books, because he craved calmness and a clear mind.

He met the most wonderful woman in the world. In her company, he wasn't always thinking about what to say, or how to be. She loved him for who he already was. The relationship cast doubt on the notion that he was unlovable.

Two daughters and marriage followed, along with two fantastic spells living and working in his beloved America.

His well-being and happiness continued to improve.

But he was still watchful, believing that well-being and happiness were the result of the right circumstances, and carefully practiced techniques.

A change in either could cause the whole house of cards to come crashing down, and when occasionally the house buckled, he assumed it was because of something he wasn't doing - he wasn't devoting enough time to the techniques or cultivating his relationships or environment.

Or that it was because of what other people were or were not doing.

He didn't want the ebbs and flows of feeling.

He wanted to feel good all the time.

He wanted to be on top form all the time.

Anything less, was not good enough.

Then one day he learned a fundamental truth about how the human experience is created.

Inspired by the teachings of Sydney Banks, he learned that no human experience is possible without the power of Thought.

What this did for him, was hugely simplify his life.

He realized that rather than being at the mercy of circumstances, situations and people, his experiences were completely created by Thought.

He could see that in those times he did not deal with things gracefully, it was because he had fallen into the trap of believing feeling was coming from somewhere other than Thought.

He came to understand that it works this way for everyone.

Because every human being experiences different thinking, they see the world differently.

No two people see the world in the exact same way.

They can hold very similar views, but there will always be differences, even if these are infinitesimal.

Seeing this helped Phil to be more empathetic. When he came across a different viewpoint, he would try to understand it, rather than immediately rejecting it.

His mental landscape began to change. Long held beliefs began to crumble.

Over the next few years, his head became an increasingly quiet place as more and more preoccupations, assumptions and beliefs were shown to be thoughts masquerading as truths.

Then one day it occurred to him that if anything that can ever be experienced is a thought, then that must mean that his experience of Phil was a creation of thought as well.

Otherwise, the rule of experience being one hundred percent Thought generated would not hold true.

Which led to the search to find Phil. Like the Search for Spock, but lower budget and with slightly less pointy ears.

This exploration has proven to be quite earth shattering – but in a good way.

It turns out that Phil isn't quite who he thought he was.

And neither are you.

The metaphors in this book chart the journey.

The journey is an amazingly liberating experience.

I truly hope that you enjoy these metaphors, which I use because they are a relatable way of describing the indescribable.

I hope they open up new perspectives and possibilities for whomever it is that you happen to be.

For I am willing to bet, you are not who you think you are.

EXPERIENCE IS 100% THOUGHT
CREATED

Thoughts are like shadows

Thoughts are like shadows cast by the sun - they have no reality independent of the perennial source which creates them.

As permanent as rain

Just as surely as rain dampens the ground, so thoughts create our experience.

Just as rain evaporates, so thoughts disappear from Consciousness.

We are not dampened permanently, even though it may feel that way at the time.

You don't have to buy

Thoughts are like door to door salesmen - they will always be coming around and ringing your doorbell.

You're not obliged to buy what they are selling.

The filter of thought

Thought acts on Consciousness like a filter placed on a camera lens.

The image seen through that lens is not the pure truth, but a representation, a variation of it, created by the colouring of the filter.

It is not to be taken as the truth.

The veil of thought

Just as the face of the bride is hidden behind a veil, so the true nature of every person is hidden behind a veil of thoughts and stories.

The groom who wishes to look on the face of his beloved does not go drawing a picture of a beautiful face upon the veil, he removes it.

And yet, when we go in search of our true nature, we look to add those things we believe to be missing - looks, physique, wealth, love.

In doing so, we are drawing an image of what we desire on the veil, when all that is needed is to lift the veil and look at the beautiful truth that lies beneath.

100% of the time

The Scottish theosopher Sydney Banks shared that there are three principles which describe the human experience:

Mind – the energy source which creates everything in life, and of which everything is made.

Consciousness – the capacity which enables us to be aware of life.

Thought – every feeling, perception and experience we can ever have is a creation of Thought.

These three principles are before form - whether that form be a person, an animal, a building or anything else you care to mention - and yet all forms are made of these principles in the same way that waves are made of water.

Take away any one of these capacities, and there is no experience.

What would happen if you did not have the power to think?

Football games would be really dull.

What would it be like without awareness?

Like watching a football game on television having muted the sound and making the brightness contrast as dark as possible.

And life without an energy source?

Like an unplugged television.

My friend Jamie Smart often uses this great phrase:

"Experience is 100 percent Thought taking form in the moment."

You could substitute the words "Mind" and "Consciousness" for the word "Thought", and it works just as well:

"Experience is 100 percent Consciousness taking form in the moment."

"Experience is 100 percent Mind taking form in the moment."

You may ask at this point,

"If you can substitute any one of the three principles into the sentence so easily, what's the difference between the three?"

And the answer is, there really isn't one.

Sydney Banks said as much but preferred to express the one principle as three because he believed it would make the concept easier to understand.

There is but one creative principle, expressing itself in infinite ways to create the universe and the experience of it, a principle which has been known by many names over hundreds of years by hundreds of different traditions.

The source of the light

It is easy to be mistaken in assuming the source of things.

For example, we often enjoy the sight of our garden bathed in the ethereal glow of moonlight.

As much as it may look as though the light is coming from the moon, it's not.

The light apparently projected from the moon is really sunlight reflecting off the moon.

As humans we are often unhappy because we believe our feelings are coming from other people, events and situations, rather than from thoughts.

That's like believing the moon is the source of moonlight.

Just as removing the sun would throw our garden into darkness even if the moon remained, so taking away our ability to be conscious and to think would remove experience, even if the people, situations and events were still there.

11

Whenever life gets you down, question the source of your feelings - are they really coming from where you think they are?

The illusion of control

We cannot control the weather.

We cannot control the coming and going of day and night.

The passing of the seasons.

The waves in the ocean.

We have switches to turn a lamp on and off, knobs which we turn to fire up the oven to cook a meal, an ignition to start and stop the car.

The mind has no switches or knobs with which to stem the flow of thinking.

Why do we believe we can control thoughts?

We no more own thinking than a lamp owns electricity, than a car engine owns the spark which starts it.

As long as we move around on this earth, thinking is inevitable, and it comes to mind whether we want it to or not.

Thinking is never personal, and we cannot own it, even when we may fervently believe that we do.

Why pretend it is yours?

We all think differently

It's not difficult to prove we live in a world of thought.

Go survey a group of people about any controversial topic you care to think of and ask them to rate its impact on a scale of 1-10, where 1 is not at all, and 10 is completely.

For example, you might ask,

"How damaging is global warming to the planet?"

"To what degree is social media a negative influence on your life?"

"To what extent will leaving the European Union be a good thing for Britain?"

Ask a dozen people and the numbers they respond with will be varied.

Ask a thousand people, and the responses will be even more varied.

If there were any intrinsic value to the event, all the numbers given would be exactly the same.

But they are not.

Why?

Because we all think differently.

Innate ability

There is an old story:

"The centipede was happy, quite!
Until a toad in fun, said:
'Pray, which leg goes after which?'
This worked his mind to such a pitch,
He lay distracted in a ditch,
Considering how to run."

The centipede quite happily placed many legs in front of many other legs with nary a danger of tripping up.

As soon as the centipede began to think about it, to consciously take command of the movements, it all became a terrible mess.

How many thousands of vital operations are going on in our bodies every day which we never give the slightest attention to?

The beating of the heart, the in and out of the breath, the cell regeneration which ensures we periodically have an entirely new body?

How much conscious effort do such operations usually take on our part?

Why is it when planning, problem solving or taking action that we often believe we must rely solely on intellect?

Doesn't the evidence of our everyday life suggest otherwise?

I'm not suggesting the intellect is not useful. That it can or should be ignored.

It can be incredibly helpful.

I'm simply noting that left to its own devices, our innate essence is capable of some pretty amazing things. It keeps us alive, for a start. It enables us to know we are alive. It enables us to experience.

Without it, intellect does not exist.

What happens when we are open to the possibility that this innate essence is capable of coming to the perfect solution, without our help?

A Beautiful Mind

The movie *A Beautiful Mind* tells the story of John Nash, a scientist who numbered among his achievements a Nobel Prize in Economics for his work on game theory.

Nash's brilliance wins him a prize scholarship to Princeton University to study mathematics. While there, he develops a new concept of governing dynamics, which earns him an appointment at the prestigious Massachusetts Institute of Technology. Some years later, he is invited to the Pentagon to help crack coded messages intercepted from the Russians.

Part of the film explores the key influences of his college roommate Charles Herman and Nash's mysterious supervisor at the Pentagon, William Parcher.

Charles is a consistent presence and source of counsel, influencing Nash in many ways – notably in persuading him to propose to his girlfriend.

Parcher asks Nash to decode messages hidden in magazines and newspapers which detail a Soviet plot.

Nash becomes increasingly obsessive about this search and believes that he is being followed.

When giving a lecture at Harvard University, Nash tries to flee from people he believes are Soviet agents. He is restrained, sedated and placed under the care of psychiatrist Dr. Rosen, who tells Nash's wife Alicia a difficult truth – that Charles and Parcher are hallucinations dreamt up by Nash.

While we may not dream up people in the way Nash does, do we ever see people as they truly are?

Or do we simply see a thought created representation of them?

Thought can be so convincing that we begin to solidify a picture of who people are and what they are like – we define them as attractive, thin, funny.

We often completely overlook changes in their physique, or behaviour.

If we do notice them, we may rationalize the changes by believing it's "out of character" for the person, forgetting their "character" was something we made up in the first place!

The character of everyone is forever in flux. Changes might be evident; they may be imperceptible. But they are evolving, changing in countless ways, moment by moment.

We never see the real person, we only ever see a thought created representation of them.

We can never know how accurate these representations are, for they are not a true depiction of the subject, merely a momentary perspective.

Realizing our perceptions of others are thought generated enables us to not take those perceptions quite as seriously.

To not feel such turbulent emotions about folk.

Realizing that the perceptions of other people are generated in the same way promotes empathy.

We are all walking around in our own thought generated realities, doing what makes sense to us in the moment, given the thinking we are experiencing in that moment.

Thinking is temporary, transitory. It changes in an instant.

And as it does, so does our worldview.

New vistas are not only possible, they are inevitable.

Virtual Reality

Imagine being in a war-torn country.

Bloodied and weary from fighting insurgents, you stealthily advance across the roof of the compound where you know the hostages are being held.

Suddenly you are jumped from the side.

You grapple with your assailant, and a mighty struggle ensues, until finally you are able to grab his lapels and throw him over the side of the building.

You resume edging your way towards the door, now conscious of a nagging pain in your right foot from raining kicks on your attacker.

As you do so, you become aware of someone softly calling your name.

The voice is oddly familiar, but out of place. You ignore it and continue on your way.

But the voice repeats your name again and again, becoming increasingly louder and more insistent.

Removing the virtual reality goggles, you see the face of your beautiful wife.

A face rather flushed with bemusement as she looks at you from her place on the living room couch.

Following her gaze, you see the smashed vase and the bouquet of flowers strewn across the floor.

You see the over-turned coffee table and realize why your right foot is throbbing.

At least that part wasn't imagined.

Well, that's what you think.

Life is like virtual reality.

We don't experience facts. We experience thoughts.

And that's a big difference.

What we are thinking might be true, but then again, it might not.

The tabloid journalist

Thought is like a tabloid journalist.

A situation can be sensationalised, an entire story based on a vague photograph or an isolated comment from a ninety-minute conversation.

Things can be viewed in ways which provide an entirely new meaning.

How closely the story relates to reality will be wildly variable.

Yet, the reader can be enraptured by what is read, convinced this depiction is the truth.

They can become outraged, stressed, have arguments, engage in feuds, all because of how they have interpreted the story presented to them.

They may take actions which influence thousands of others for good or bad.

Look at the media coverage of the Trump administration, the Duke and Duchess of Sussex's withdrawal from Royal life, the COVID-19 pandemic.

What is written about these subjects is variable.

Some of it may be quite accurate and some of it, pure fiction.

But what is written shapes the opinions and perceptions of millions of people.

People do not react to what is true.

They react to what seems believable.

And so it is with thought.

We cannot know how true thought is, but it is all we know.

It can be compelling.

Because we all think differently, we can be polarised, even when discussing the same people and events, because thought is the ultimate tabloid journalist.

Let it flow!

Whenever you are feeling overwhelmed or simply just don't like your thinking, remember that thoughts are like the water in a washbasin.

If the water becomes dirty, it's not a comment on the nature of the basin.

If you want fresh water, you don't try to clean the dirty droplets.

You simply remove the plug, turn on the taps and allow fresh water to flow.

Similarly, you don't need to fix or manage your thoughts.

No thought defines the person it passes through.

Thoughts are always flowing, and because of that, fresh thought is inevitable.

Fishing for thoughts

We catch thoughts as an expert fisherman catches carp.

The fisherman wades into the stream, waits, gets a bite, hauls it in, weighs it and takes photos.

And then releases the carp back into the stream.

The fisherman knows that he does not own the stream or the fish.

He recognizes that by keeping the fish, he would be disturbing the natural balance of the ecosystem.

He is aware that the nature of the stream is to flow, and the nature of the carp is to swim in that stream.

We go fishing in the stream of Consciousness for thoughts.

We wait – but not too long – for a bite. We grab one, haul it in and begin weighing it up.

We take photos from every conceivable angle.

But then – unlike the fisherman – we do not release the thought.

We take it home, fillet, cook, and consume it and frequently, suffer after-effects.

We forget that the nature of thought is to swim effortlessly through Consciousness.

We forget that we neither own thought, nor are we defined by it.

Thinking doesn't have to sting

Being convinced the thinking which assails you is bound to hurt is like a trainee beekeeper not realizing they are allowed protective clothing.

The beekeeper might be fearful of the bees, convinced they will be swarmed, attacked and badly hurt.

But once they put on protective clothing, the keeper can work with the bees and observe them in complete safety.

They can become absorbed in the bees, fascinated by them and their lives, knowing they do not have to feel endangered.

Similarly - as we come to see that thinking is not a factual commentary on our personal situation but a momentary perception of the world around us - it changes our relationship to thinking.

We see that we need not fear thoughts.

Rather than being in the thrall of thoughts, we are the observer of them.

The observer which the thoughts are experienced within.

The bees may be outside the beekeeper's clothing, but they are also experienced within the beekeeper's thinking.

And when you understand bees, and understand thinking, both are far less likely to sting.

What swings the pendulum?

When I was small, my mum would sing me the nursery rhyme:

"Hickory Dickory Dock,
The mouse ran up the clock,
The clock struck one,
The mouse ran down,
Hickory Dickory Dock."

We are like a mouse clinging to the pendulum of the grandfather clock, wanting to be spared all the back and forth, spending our time developing strategies to slow the pendulum, or to get off it, so we can gain control of our movements.

But what if we were to question what swings the pendulum?

Journeying upwards to the source of the swing, we would find that the movement of the pendulum – once set in motion - is governed by the natural laws of weight and gravity.

We can interfere with that motion, but the pendulum is inclined to keep moving without our help.

As human beings, we like to believe we are responsible for our experience.

But when we look to the source, we will see that the source of all experience is thought.

It is thought that swings the pendulum of life, and always will.

Whether we choose to accept that or continue to struggle against it - well that's thought, too.

Because thought is all there is to experience.

The Game of Life

As we see that our experience of life is completely a creation of thought, and that this is the same for everyone, we may come to see life as a series of never-ending games.

We may also come to see how arbitrary and made up the rules of these games are.

But even if we do not like the rules, if we want to win these games it does us no good to ignore the rules while playing.

In the game of soccer, you can be the most prolific striker in the world, but if you hate the offside rule and don't learn to play within it, you won't score many goals.

If you want to thrive within the game, it's good to know the rules, and who the referee is.

It doesn't mean you have to agree with the rules.

It doesn't mean you have to believe in the game.

The nice thing about realizing you're in a game is you can step out of it anytime and go play a different one.

Thought in the moment

A few years back a good friend sent me a note to tell me that she had been in a car accident with her husband.

He did not survive.

As I read her message, I began to shake with despair. For some time, I could not grasp a thought, being consumed with feeling for my friend and her loss.

The next day I was much calmer and less embattled by these thoughts.

But as I worked, I began to dwell on how my friend had been prematurely deprived of her love, of how unfair it all was.

In no time at all, I had gone from feeling relatively calm, to feeling as though I had a lead balloon in my stomach.

Then I had a presentation to do, and as I shared my head cleared and the balloon disappeared.

Reflecting on this experience, I was shocked at how my feeling state had fluctuated.

When the accident actually happened, I was blissfully unaware and very happy.

When I found out about it, I reacted as though the accident had happened in that moment.

While my feeling state fluctuated wildly over the next few days, the outward circumstances had not changed – the accident and its fatal consequences were a fact, and nothing would change that, as much as I might wish that something could.

While we often believe otherwise, we can only ever experience thought in this moment.

And in that there is great hope – no matter what the circumstances, thoughts and feelings can and will change, and as they do, so does our perspective of the world.

Suspect judgment

When things are not going the way we want them to, we look for a culprit.

Like a detective, we investigate, following up leads, clues and tips to establish a list of suspects.

We then whittle this list down until we pass judgment on the most likely guilty party.

It's interesting that when looking for a culprit, we search through our experience but tend not to question what is creating that experience.

What we do find when we do?

That every experience is composed of thought.

That nothing can be experienced without thought.

Why do we miss this?

Thought is so all-encompassing that we tend not to notice it. Instead, we focus on the apparent separation between us and everything else.

We tend not to notice that experience is one seamless whole made of thought.

No other suspects need to be considered.

All other avenues of inquiry can be eliminated.

And as a result, the mind is cleared.

Is separation drummed into you?

Thought can beguile us into believing that experience is separate from thinking.

But how is it possible to have any experience without thought being involved?

What can you know without thought?

Thought creates our experience of the world; it creates our experience of the person we believe ourselves to be.

It is the source of all experience.

Thought and experience are one – there is no separation.

Believing otherwise, is like believing the drumbeat is separate from the drum and the one who sounds it.

It's not about addition

Many people rely on strategies or techniques to think or feel better.

This reliance demonstrates a fundamental misunderstanding about how humans work.

It suggests we are in some way lacking.

It shows we are caught up in the situation.

But feelings and perceptions of ourselves and the situations we find ourselves in, are only ever creations of thought.

Adding thinking to solve a thought created problem only compounds matters.

If you are trying to find a pair of socks in a drawer, do you throw more socks on top before you begin to search?

If it's a hot day, do you put a sweater on to cool down?

Don't try to add.

Realize that problems are not symptomatic of the situation but a consequence of how we relate to thinking.

Strategies and techniques are not necessary to manage thought or feeling, because these change just as surely as one movie frame follows another.

One morning I awoke with a horrible pressure on my chest.

My mind raced as I tried to think what it might be.

Chronic indigestion?

Heart attack?

I opened my eyes to see a furry face staring back.

My cat had curled up on my chest and fallen asleep.

I didn't need to add anything to feel better.

I just needed to subtract a cat.

What lies beneath the waves of thought?

You can be swimming in a calm ocean. Suddenly a storm kicks up and you are being tossed and turned, battered by the tumbling waves and struggling for breath.

In this moment, there are options.

Continue to struggle and exhaust yourself, leaving yourself less able to swim to shore when the storm abates.

You can stop struggling and allow the waves to take you where they will. It might not be pleasant, but at the very least, you'll be conserving energy.

Or you can dive under the waves, to a place which is calm and tranquil, while the storm rages on the surface.

Mentally, you can be suddenly caught in a thought storm.

It's easy to be overwhelmed, to believe the thoughts are a commentary on your situation.

On who you are.

You might take ownership of these thoughts.

You could fight them.

Or, you may choose to ride the thought storm out. You might not like the thoughts, but you don't have to own them. You can recognize that these thoughts are neither yours, nor a narrative about you.

You could ask:

"What lies beneath these thoughts?"

We are not the thoughts we experience, and thought does not change our true nature.

Who we are, is that which lies beneath thought.

An impartial recorder

Who we truly are works like a tape recorder, recording every experience, thought and feeling.

It just accepts whatever is imprinted on it, it does not judge, evaluate or emote over any of the content.

It does not identify with what it records.

Who we truly are does not identify with any experience, thought or feeling.

It does not identify with anything that is created, even though it is, itself, the creator of everything.

NO THOUGHT IS TRUE

Always a gem

Identifying with thinking instead of our true nature is like owning a diamond covered in dirt.

Does being covered in dirt make it any less the diamond?

We can get so obsessed with the dirt that we forget the diamond.

We can expend a lot of energy trying to clean the diamond, reassuring ourselves it is still there.

Or, we can just remember that it is a diamond, no matter what the temporary covering may be.

What is constant in experience?

In the great spiritual text, the *Tripura Rahasya*, it is written:

"Truth can never change its nature, whereas untruth is always changing."

If this is true, then what I truly am must be unchanging.

Does my thinking change?

Do my feelings change?

Does my body change?

Since they do, none of these can be what I truly am.

Whatever I am, must be a constant in experience.

What is a constant in experience, ever present in every moment?

What is the origin?

The legendary Indian sage Siddharameswar Maharaj told the story of Gomaji Ganesh, who, living in the town of Andheri, established the convention that no order or document could be accepted as legal unless it bore the stamp, "Gomaji Ganesh, The Brass Door".

From then on, officials of the town only accepted documents if they bore this stamp. The stamp became part of the official legal system of Andheri.

One day, a case cited a document which was legal in all senses apart from bearing this obligatory stamp.

An objection was raised that because the document lacked this stamp it should be disqualified as evidence, but a courageous man argued the document should be admissible because the stamp was the only missing legality.

The stamp became a bone of contention.

It was decided the legality of the stamp should be examined.

The judge in the case took on this inquiry himself, discovering that Gomaji Ganesh was a man of no particular status or authority who had taken advantage of the badly administered government of many years past, putting his name on the stamp that was used for all official business.

Thereafter, the tradition of applying his stamp was followed blindly by succeeding government officials.

Once the truth of its origin was discovered, the stamp was rejected and viewed with ridicule.

How often we are so beguiled by accepted beliefs that it doesn't occur to us to inquire about their authenticity or origin!

We are fascinated by the Brooklyn Bridge, but less inquisitive about the bricks, mortar, cables, craftsmen and architect that were integral to its creation.

But we cannot ignore the source if we want to know the truth of something.

That would be like asking someone to pass a golden vase without touching the gold.

We are very accepting of beliefs, particularly if they are widely held.

"All politicians are corrupt."

"Society demands that I be this way."

"Exams are stressful."

My eldest daughter has always questioned things, and I love her for that inclination.

I remember her telling me of a discussion at school where the question posed to the class was,

"What caused The Big Bang?"

The consensus answer was a speck of dust.

But rather than accept the popular answer, my daughter asked another question:

"If the speck of dust was the beginning of everything, where did the speck of dust come from?"

If we are interested in truth, we need to inquire more. To find out through our own experience, rather than taking the words of others for granted.

To ask, how true is this belief, really?

What is its true origin?

Whatever your answers to these questions, ask – are those answers really true?

I'm finding the more I question, the less I'm certain, the less that appears true to me.

And while some may find that frightening, to me it is liberating.

It means there are less and less limitations in life and more possibilities.

I know that some are afraid to question, because of what they may learn - it's the fear of the unknown, and that's very understandable.

But here's the thing about the fear of the unknown:

What do we ever know, really?

We can't tell the future, although we often like to pretend that we can.

If we could, wouldn't things turn out the way we guess they will, every single time?

Wouldn't we be winning the lottery every week?

Truth is, we live our whole lives in the unknown.

Whether you believe that or not, that's the way it is, so why fight it?

One of the biggest beliefs we hold is the one of who I am.

Irrespective of your name, your relationships, your job and your station in life - what are the origins of your identity?

Where is your identity located?

Whose stamp do you bear?

How authentic is it, really?

What is true is unchanging

What is true can never change its nature, and that which changes cannot be true.

Thoughts are continually changing, being replaced by other thoughts, moment to moment.

So how true can they be?

Thoughts are like the images of a camera - momentary representations of the world. Take another shot a second later and the image captured may be completely different.

Because they are always changing, thoughts are not true.

To that idea you might object,

"I love my children. Are you telling me that's not true?"

No, I'm not.

I'm saying, what the thought describes may be true, but the thought isn't, because the thought is a representation, a label, a best attempt to describe what it refers to.

The thought is not the thing it attempts to capture.

Believing that thoughts are a true depiction of the world, is like believing that because you have seen the portrait of the Mona Lisa you know the woman in the picture.

We think we know, but we don't. We can't. We can guess, but really we have no idea how close to the truth those guesses are.

And this can be freeing, because we come to realize that we do not see the world as it is.

We see a version of the world that is created by thought.

And because thoughts are always changing, a new experience is inevitable.

As much as it may feel otherwise, we are not trapped by any situation, feeling, or persons, because our experience of these are not truths, they are a snapshot made of thinking.

No thought definitively describes who we are, what our circumstances might be, or speaks to the state of any of our relationships.

No thought is true.

The paintbrush of Thought

The world-renowned artist picks up his brush, and begins to paint, just as he has thousands of times before.

He is known for the feeling, the texture and the meaning he brings to the work. For the dazzling contrasts of colour, perspectives, the subtle use of light.

Sometimes the work he produces is easily recognizable, identifiable and relatable.

Sometimes it has viewers scratching their head, unable to understand what impression the artist is trying to convey.

Sometimes the work creates much admiration, but it has also been known to create controversy, argument, even revulsion.

Regardless, the artist continues to allow the brush to do its work, to see what is produced.

He knows that whatever the result – whether the work inspires, causes controversy, or some other reaction - the output of the work is not the truth, merely a representation of it.

The artist is Consciousness.

The brush, Thought.

A while ago I was in Barcelona, a beautiful city awash in culture and art, and my wanderings took me to the Picasso museum.

The work displayed formed a chronology of his development as an artist, and I was fascinated to see how his style evolved over time, from classically conventional in his teens to the more challenging works of his later years, with body parts stretched, multiplied and liberally strewn across the canvas as though Picasso were creating a human casserole.

At some point in his development Picasso clearly thought to himself about classical depiction,

"I'm bored with this. I'm going to look at it another way." (But in Spanish).

Here was a man who knew he could not depict truth. But he could produce a perspective on it.

His life's work seemed devoted to addressing fascinating questions such as:

- There are many ways of looking at this, everyone sees it differently, why be limited to a single perspective? That perspective might be accepted by the mainstream as the most realistic, but does that make it true?

- Life is a series of momentary impressions, fleeting, gone before you can appreciate them. Why be limited, defined by them?

So often people get lost in convention, in belief that things should be a certain way.

They forget that in life all experience is the result of thought dancing across the canvas of Consciousness, and that the effect, no matter how inspiring, or moving, is momentary.

They forget that while thought may be the sole creator of experience, it is not true.

It is a perspective.

The invisible media

Why do we dwell on our thoughts, rather than our true nature?

For the same reason we focus on the words in the newspaper, and not what the newspaper is made from.

The newspaper is made from paper and ink. But really we only notice how the ink is arranged on the page, arranged into the words which make up stories.

Our interpretation of these words creates emotional reactions which can be positive, negative or neutral.

There is no innate truth in these words. Our reaction to them is dictated by thought.

We simply find the words more interesting than the paper on which they are printed.

And why wouldn't we?

The paper always appears to be the same, while the words are always changing.

But without the paper, the words have nothing in which to appear.

Thoughts are always changing, and because of that seem more interesting than that in which they appear.

But just because something is interesting, doesn't make it true.

Belief in the truth of anything can lead to identification with it.

Once identification with anything happens, limitation occurs.

It is easy to believe we are defined by our experience of thoughts.

We can get so caught up in these that we don't notice they are always changing.

We also tend to be oblivious to the unchanging background in which our thoughts appear.

The unchanging background that has to be present in order for us to have any experience.

What is the unchanging background in which every experience appears?

Who is it perfect to?

Often in life I have been hindered by a tendency towards perfectionism.

This has manifested itself in different ways in different arenas.

At work, one of the ways it would play out would be in my approach towards deadlines.

With two weeks to prepare a PowerPoint presentation for a manager, I would spend thirteen of the fourteen days grinding away, second, third and fourth guessing my slides as I sought to reach PowerPoint Valhalla.

Those thirteen days tended to not be that pleasant. My head would be like a big city marathon, with hundreds of thoughts running around, jostling for position, striving to be first to the finish line.

The race would often continue long into the night.

Invariably, I would submit something I was less than happy with. It would get returned with numerous correction and amendment requests, with very little time to make the changes before the presentation was due to be shared.

One day, the question popped into my head,

"When you have perfected this, who is it perfect to?"

And the answer - delivered rather sheepishly – was:

"Me."

And me alone.

While the presentation might look good to me, to others it might be complete trash.

There is no guaranteed way of knowing what other people will think, because everyone thinks differently.

As this realization sunk into my cranium like a jasmine bath bomb dissolving into the hot water, I began to relax.

It occurred to me that if my presentations were going to be less than perfect to some no matter what I did, I could achieve less than perfect in less time.

Rather than striving for perfection, I did what made sense, what looked good enough to me and trusted the manager would tell me what needed changing.

I began to submit the presentation drafts earlier, to allow more time for review, for changes to be requested and made.

This proved less stressful and more efficient, and I freed up lots of time for other things. The marathon runners of thought in my head departed, replaced by a smattering of relaxed dog walkers.

And the funny thing is, I began getting fewer corrections and better reviews for presentations.

The experience of thought is not the experience of truth.

It is the experience of a perspective.

A perspective which can vary according to the moment and the perceiver.

No matter how well we know others, we can never know exactly what they are thinking.

We can only know our thought created experience of them.

Perfection is a comparative perspective - a concept that varies from person to person and moment to moment – and because of this, it doesn't help to crank the wheel of perfection.

We can only do what makes sense in the moment, and then see what happens.

The instrument of Thought

Watch jazz musicians in an improvisation and you will see a group of people lost in the moment, with musical notes being freely expressed and experienced without judgment, concern about their meaning or their impact on the overall piece.

The musicians' experiment, knowing they cannot anticipate what might be learned or produced until the music is over. They recognize they do not own the notes, which are an expression of the infinitely creative energy that is the bedrock of all life.

In everyday life, thoughts tend to be treated very differently from the way a jazz musician treats notes. Thoughts are imbued with meaning, seen to have something meaningful to say about who we are, our relationships and the situations in our lives.

But really, thoughts are like jazz notes. They come to us, pass through us and then fade away, to be replaced by the next ones.

No one owns, or controls, thoughts.

No thought has any intrinsic meaning, and no thought can capture who we truly are.

Just keep on playing, recognizing that thoughts are momentary expressions and not the truth which lies before any rendition that we care to give, musical or not!

Inhabiting beliefs

It's interesting how we identify with habits, and the meaning we ascribe to those habits.

Take one of the world's greatest ever tennis players, Rafael Nadal.

Before every point, he goes through an elaborate routine of toweling down, then nips, tucks and pinches various body parts.

He does this from superstition, believing that not going through the routine will bring bad luck.

But if the habit worked, wouldn't he win every point, game, set, match and tournament?

That he doesn't suggests his results are not dependent on that habit.

When the points are being played, he has no time to think about how his shorts or his hair may be hanging.

He is simply in the flow of the point, instinctively moving to where the ball will go, reacting to the bounce, and returning it.

He's rather good at this. He wins quite a lot. More than most who have ever held a racquet.

But there are times when he loses.

During those times, his approach to the game may be the same, or different.

But win or lose, the outcome is not dictated by the habit.

If you feel under the spell of a habit, take a look at it.

Is it something you are doing twenty four hours a day?

I'm guessing there are times when you are not.

I'm guessing there are times when you don't even think about it.

I'm guessing that sometimes the habit is helpful and other times it isn't.

That sometimes you are successful without the habit and sometimes not.

There's a reason for this.

You are not the habit.

Your success and failure are not dependent on that habit.

You are not defined by the habit, even though it may feel as though you are.

Whatever justifications you present for why the habit is unavoidable, what evidence can you come up with to prove the habit has an existence beyond the realms of thinking?

Thinking creates our world but does not define it.

Thoughts are not truths.

We are beyond habits.

We are beyond thoughts.

What is it that is beyond both?

You stupid maple tree!

My good friend Amy Johnson tells the story of how she would use the phrase:

"You stupid maple tree!"

to demonstrate to her kids that you shouldn't believe everything you're told.

If someone calls you a stupid maple tree, you don't believe it because it seems ridiculous. You are not a maple tree. You know that and every one of your acquaintance knows that.

But if someone calls you a stupid human, that looks plausible. You are a human, and maybe the stupid bit is right, too.

But what is it that makes one idea look ridiculous and another plausible?

When you were born did you know that you were a human?

Or that you were not a maple tree?

At what point did you know those things?

Wasn't it sometime after you began to learn language?

At some point after you began to be educated in the ways of the world?

Clearly from birth, we experience very powerful emotions.

But they are fleeting, and because we have yet to develop a sense of identity, we do not own them.

As we grow and learn, the world begins to be divided into opposites -

This is good, this is bad.

This is beautiful, this is ugly.

This is right, this is wrong.

This is plausible, this is implausible.

This is you. This is not you.

We begin to create a framework by which to make sense of the world.

We begin to form ideas of the way the world should be, and the way the world shouldn't be.

We create a sense of identity and begin to evaluate everything by how it relates to that sense of identity.

And the more we do this, the more we seem to own the emotions we experience.

We can be convinced that our view of the world is completely accurate and that our situation and feelings are being completely determined by it.

We can forget that our worldview is momentary, constructed not of truths and facts but from impressions, ideas and concepts.

A worldview that is entirely based in thought.

We are not limited to being a human, or a maple tree, stupid or otherwise.

We are not limited to being anything else you care to mention.

We are that which is prior to all concepts, thoughts and experiences – and because of that, we cannot be defined by anything.

Humans are a bit dim

Imagine an ornate, beautiful lamp, whose powerful translucent bulb brilliantly illuminates everything in the room.

Now imagine gently tinting that bulb a fractionally darker shade to change the light.

A tiny change in the tint will not do much to change the bulb's glow.

But tint it an increasingly darker shade and sooner or later you will be cast into darkness.

And yet the light encased in the bulb continues to shine just as brightly.

We have merely lost sight of it, because of the tinting.

To experience the full effects of the bulb, we wouldn't paint a translucent colour over the darkened tint, we would remove the darkened tint.

As human beings, we are a manifestation of the creative potential.

But as we grow, develop and learn, that creative potential gets tinted in thought.

Like the bulb, it can become dimmed to the point where we are no longer aware of it.

But the creative potential is always there - we simply need to see past the temporary covering of thought.

We simply need to uncover what has been there, all along.

Where are the boundaries of experience?

Renowned Zen master Suzuki Roshi said the best way to control a cow was to give it a very big field.

The theory being, the bigger the field, the less likely the cow is to try and escape.

How true is this in our own experience?

When we are stressed, we feel confined, the space we inhabit seems small and is possibly getting smaller by the second.

But what happens when we question these sensed boundaries?

Does it look as though these are anything other than thought?

How can you know of these boundaries, if not through thought?

Thinking has to be involved, otherwise you could not know of these boundaries.

If these boundaries are thought creations and if no thought is true, then these boundaries can't be true, either.

As it is seen that these boundaries are not real, we realize we don't need to escape from experience.

Because experience is boundless.

Experience is limitless.

It cannot confine you, and it cannot define you.

I AM A THOUGHT

The name of water

Rivers are named and you can learn of their history and character through reading or hearing stories about them.

But look at a river without knowing anything about it and you will simply see riverbanks, floating detritus, maybe some swans, and water.

You will notice the water is perpetually flowing, mud is being dislodged from the riverbank, and then it disperses with the current. The swans cut swathes through the water which leave a momentary wake before disappearing.

The river is forever changing.

As individuals we are given names, and on the surface it appears that we stay the same. But like the river, we are always changing - thoughts flow like a river current, our ideas about life are being revised, our bodies and cells, continually changing.

While we pretend otherwise, we are a momentary experience, with no more solidity or permanence to our identity than that of the river.

The shape of sand

We are like sand made into castles, which becomes so enamoured of the shape it has been sculpted into that it forgets it is sand and thinks of itself as the castle.

Sand can be made into an infinite number of shapes and forms.

Then remade, resculpted, again and again.

The sand is not limited to the form of the sculpture.

Whatever form the sand takes has no effect on its true nature.

Just as sand is sculpted into castles, so the energy from which we are made is sculpted into the human form.

That form is not fixed.

We are remade over and over as we grow and develop, as our bodies change shape, as our cells are replaced, again and again.

Why pretend we are limited to a single form?

Why pretend we are limited to a certain experience of life?

Why claim ownership of an identity which is as permanent as a sandcastle?

Before identity

What is true is unchanging, and that which changes cannot be true.

Therefore, who we truly are has to be unchanging.

Imagine you have amnesia.

Stripped of every possible form of identification, what remains?

Would there not remain a sense of aliveness?

A sense of presence?

A sense of being?

Might that be who you truly are?

Through the looking glass

Why is it difficult to know who we truly are?

For the same reason that your reflection in the mirror cannot know you.

The reflection is not the creator, the reflection is what is created.

It has no existence separate from the object and the mirror that reflects it.

Similarly, you do not create Consciousness and Thought.

You are the reflection of Consciousness and Thought, the reflection which believes in an existence separate from those elements.

Where else is there?

There is only one moment in which you can live.

Now.

There is only one place you can inhabit.

Here.

Put them together, and this is where your personal self is truly to be found -

Nowhere.

Swimming through thought

One of my daughters' idols growing up was the brilliant American swimmer, Missy Franklin.

The documentary *Touch the Wall* traces her growth from a thirteen year old phenomenon to the realization of her dreams at the London Olympics in 2012.

It portrays Missy as a carefree teenager swimming because she loves to, unburdened by commitments, thoughts about how to swim fast, or what swimming says about her as a person.

She just swims, and the medals and world records that follow are a testimony to how good she is at it.

When interviewed, she charmingly denies being famous. She genuinely cannot understand the fuss. She doesn't see anything unusual about herself.

But just four years later, Missy had slipped from the summit of World Swimming.

Although part of the USA freestyle relay team that took home gold from the Rio Olympics, she did not swim in the final, replaced by team-mates who were faster and more in-form.

What happened?

Why would someone with so much talent, and the world at their feet, lose their form so precipitously?

Her autobiography, *Relentless Spirit*, provides some tantalizing clues.

The first half of the book, which tells her story from childhood to standing on the London podium five times, is filled with the same sense of wonder, ease and enjoyment that characterized her personality in *Touch the Wall*.

But the second half paints a difference picture.

Gone is the carefree teenager who loved swimming, replaced by a careworn, injury-prone athlete burdened by expectation and endorsement dollars.

The tone is intense. The sense is one of struggle. The reader can feel the pressure she feels.

When she began to be paid to swim, Missy's thinking changed.

Swimming went from being a labour of love to a job.

She went from swimming for herself, to swimming for others.

She felt if she didn't produce results that she was letting her sponsors down.

It seemed to her the money automatically meant more expectation and stress. That swimming was now a serious business and that she had to change her approach accordingly.

She bought into the identity of Missy Franklin, obliged to produce world beating performances, because that was what she was paid for.

She did not question the truth of this identity.

We all have an identity.

But what are identities, really?

They are momentary expressions and limitations of what we truly are.

No identity is true, because identities are made of thought, and thought is too changeable to be true.

Who we are, is beyond identity.

No experience defines who we are, but it's an easy trap to fall into.

Missy came to believe she was defined by the success of her swimming.

She clearly cares deeply for society, is tireless in helping people and wanting to make the world a better place.

But – like us all – Missy is so much more than any thought or experience.

The gravity of thought

Thoughts orbit the self as the moon orbits the earth.

Anything that is experienced is experienced because of thinking, and how that thinking relates to the sense of self.

The sense of self exerts a gravitational pull on thoughts, keeping them close and making it seem as though a self owns them.

This sense of ownership causes the tumult of emotion.

But what is this sense of self made from?

Can it possibly be made of anything other than thought?

How can anything be known without thought?

If everything that can be known is a thought creation, that means the sense of self is a thought creation, too.

Can you locate any thought you have ever had?

Can you show me any thought that you have ever had?

Even the most brilliant neuroscientists cannot pinpoint the physical location of a thought.

Thought is an energy which cannot be grasped. It cannot be located.

If thought cannot be located, and the sense of self is a thought, that means the sense of self cannot be located, either.

Without thought there is no sense of self, and all thoughts are like comets, brilliantly and briefly illuminating the space of Consciousness, before disappearing to be replaced by other inexplicable wonders.

What is the ego?

When you were born, you had no idea what an ego was.

You had no sense of identity.

There was a sense of aliveness, and the experience of perceptions and emotions.

Sometimes you would cry, other times you would gurgle.

But these experiences were transitory.

As you learned language, began to build an identity, then compared that identity to the burgeoning world around you, so you developed an ego.

You delved into and believed stories - the ones you told about yourself, the ones you told about others and the world, the ones you heard or read about others, the world and yourself.

And that is what the ego is - stories.

It is the library of all the stories you have ever identified with.

The stories about you being -

A dutiful son.

A loving father.

A hopeless golfer.

A person who ought to be kinder.

Better looking.

Someone who should work harder, or not as much.

All these stories, to be found on the shelves of the library of you.

But where is this library located?

Where can I find the ego?

Can it be located in the body?

Can it be shown with a microscope?

What physical evidence have we to suggest the ego is a real thing?

The ego is made of stories.

Stories are made of thoughts.

Thoughts are too temporary to be true.

So how true can the ego be?

Where does this idea of who you are come from?

A friend walks into the room and enthusiastically greets you, spending twenty minutes asking about you and your life.

Shortly after your friend leaves, a burglar bursts in, stares at you in bewilderment, then flees.

Both the friend and the burglar see the same person, yet one instantly recognizes you, and the other has no clue.

What's the difference?

Your friend brought "you" into the room with them.

The burglar didn't.

Who you are is a different story in every person's head - including your own – and because of that, people have very different reactions to you.

If who you are is not readily obvious to everyone, then where did the idea of you come from?

Take me, as "Phil".

Which came first, "Phil" or a baby?

A baby came first. "Phil" was the name my mother and father gave that baby after it arrived.

From humble beginnings, this "Phil" gradually became embellished – this is "Phil's" body, these are "Phil's" belongings, this is "Phil's" family, this is "Phil's" house.

But these embellishments are nothing more than stories. Meaningless to anyone who does not know "Phil" or anything about "Phil".

A burglar will see house contents and a person who may be an obstacle to their intention, but they will not see a "Phil".

So who is "Phil" truly?

What is true, is constant and unchanging. Whatever changes and is inconstant, cannot be true.

Experiences of situations, relationships and places are not constant, and your remembrance of those things changes with time. So too do perceptions and feelings about yourself and other people.

Your outlook on life is continually refreshing.

Your body changes, thousands of cells are regenerating on a daily basis. You are different from one heartbeat to the next.

When I put on a bit of weight I don't celebrate, "There's more Phil!"

When I lose a bit of weight, I don't commiserate, "There's less Phil!"

What are the constants in "Phil's" human existence? What can be proven, experientially?

There is an energy which gives life.

There is a capacity which provides an awareness of this life.

There is an ability which enables interpretation of this life.

All life experiences are created by these principles.

But these principles are not operating within "Phil".

These principles exist prior to "Phil".

"Phil" is a creation of these principles.

"Phil" is these principles in action.

Where am I? (Part One)

It's become increasingly apparent to me that the source of my emotional ups and downs is a consequence of how "Phil" relates to experience.

They say if you want to effect a cure, first find the root of the problem - so let's try and find where "Phil" might be.

Let's look at the right foot.

Is this where "Phil" lives?

If it is, and that right foot is lost in an accident, does that mean "Phil" is gone?

No - so "Phil" can't be living there.

What about in the right kneecap? Or the right hip?

"Phil" can't be anywhere in the right leg, because even if it were lost, the sense of "Phil" would remain.

What about the left leg?

Again, if the left foot, knee, hip or leg were lost, the sense of "Phil" would still be present.

Now it's all very well saying that a sense of "Phil" is there, but that's no proof of an actual "Phil".

You can have a sense of an intruder in your house, but that doesn't mean there actually is one.

Having eliminated the lower half of the body as the possible residence of "Phil", let's go to the upper half.

What about the arms?

What about the torso?

What about the chest?

We will not find compelling evidence of "Phil" anywhere in those parts.

Now some might say,

"Ah, but what about the heart? Will "Phil" not be found there?"

People have heart transplants and they still have the same apparent identity.

So, where is "Phil" hiding?

What about the head?

Surely, he must be in the most recognizable part of a human being?

Well, you only know the face is mine because you have been told by me or some other source that it is the face of "Phil".

You only have my word for that.

As I only have my mother's.

My face does not announce me to those who do not know me – to them I remain anonymous.

Even if you were able to look inside my brain, you will not find any evidence of a "Phil".

For many years, I suspected if my brain were to be cracked open, you would find it being powered by a little hamster racing around a wheel in there, and that hamster might be "Phil".

But maybe not.

Look inside my brain and you will no more find the ideas of "Phil" than you can make a bed from a cloud.

You could extract my brain and show it to the doctor and he will just see a piece of grey, brainy stuff.

So, we have now done a thorough autopsy on "Phil" and not found a single trace of him.

A sense of "Phil", yes.

But no solid, irrefutable proof of the person known as "Phil".

Now - if there is no "Phil" to be found inside "his" body, where might "Phil" be found outside "his" body?

Oh dear.

He can't.

How disappointing for the wife and kids.

Where am I? (Part Two)

Imagine you are in a court of law.

It's your fantasy, so you can make the reason you are before the judge as exciting or as trivial as you like.

The judge asks you to show proof of your identity.

What evidence will you provide?

It will be something like a driver's licence, or a passport, right? Because those are the official documents that prove who you are.

But what proof of identity did you use to get those documents?

Maybe you used your passport to get your driver's licence.

What did you use to get your passport?

I would imagine it was your birth certificate.

Now, what evidence was provided to validate the identity recorded on the birth certificate?

Your birth certificate was based on the word of your parents, wasn't it?

How did they know your name?

They made it up, didn't they?

My mother didn't give birth to a "Phil".

She gave birth to a baby.

The biography of "Phil" began sometime later, with first the inscription of his name, and then the creation of his identity via the innumerable entries made subsequently by "Phil" and the people "Phil" encountered.

These stories, from which his identity is constructed, are all made of thoughts.

Thoughts which are not truths.

The stories and thoughts about "Phil" are not the true self, because what is true never changes.

What "Phil" truly is, is beyond the name, the body and the experiences.

Who is really behind the curtain?

When we first hear of the Wizard in *The Wizard of Oz*, we learn of a sorcerer with an awesome reputation. The ruler of The Emerald City, he is believed to be capable of miracles.

It is to him that Dorothy and her friends are directed when they speak to others of their hearts' desires - Dorothy wants to go home, the Lion is desperate for courage, the Tin Man yearns for a heart and the Scarecrow would love a brain.

Their first meeting with the Wizard is an intimidating experience. He has a visage of gigantic proportions, a booming, commanding voice, and his image is enhanced by spectacular pyrotechnics.

Because of the awe, fear and respect he inspires, Dorothy and her friends have no hesitation in following his instructions to the letter to get what they want.

But it's all an illusion. When Dorothy's dog Toto pulls back the curtain, the Wizard is revealed to be an ordinary, little old man. The Wizard they believed in, is machine generated.

We too project a personality, an image of who we are, both to ourselves and all those who come into contact with us.

So convincing is this projection, we often buy into it ourselves, believing it to be who we truly are.

Our self-image can bring much joy, and much misery.

But it is not the limits of who we are.

Before Dorothy goes back to Kansas, Glinda the Good Witch tells her she always did have the power to return home. She just had to learn it for herself.

Hearing this, Dorothy reflects:

"If I ever go looking for my heart's desire again, I won't look any further than my own backyard. Because if it isn't there, I never really lost it to begin with."

What you are looking for is closer than close, and never anything other than what you already are.

More than a part

Sean Connery will always be remembered for playing James Bond.

Daniel Radcliffe will forever be Harry Potter.

Tom Baker, synonymous with Doctor Who.

Dame Maggie Smith - take your pick from Jean Brodie, Professor McGonagall, Lady Violet Crawley and a host of other characters.

But however brilliantly these actors inhabit their parts, they are not defined by them.

Going through life pretending that our character is fixed, is like Dame Maggie Smith believing she is limited to being Lady Violet Crawley.

A wonderful part it is true, but not the sum-total of who she is.

She is so much more.

Just as we are so much more than the parts we play - the husband, the father, the brother, the friend, the employee.

These are but momentary incarnations of our true essence.

Just as Lady Violet Crawley is an expression of Dame Maggie Smith, so we and all the roles we play are an expression of the infinitely creative energy which animates all life.

Sweeping changes

There are many fabulous jokes in the classic British sitcom *Only Fools and Horses*.

One of my favourites is when the hapless Trigger announces that he has won an award from the Council. Working as a road sweep, he has been recognized for keeping the same broom for eighteen years.

He proudly says,

"In all that time, it's only had ten new handles and six new heads."

We laugh, because we know it's not really the same broom. The parts have been switched out numerous times and there's nothing left of the original.

But when it comes to ourselves, we absolutely identify with the body. We completely overlook that since birth, not only have we grown, and shrunk, but our attitudes and perspectives have changed, and every cell in our body has switched out many times over.

Just because our physiology looks roughly the same day to day doesn't mean that it is.

We are different people, day to day, moment to moment, breath to breath, one heartbeat to the next.

Where is this self that we identify so closely with?

The one who suffers, feels elation, who dares, who wins, who loses, who wakes and sleeps?

You might point the person out to me and say, "There they are."

But point them out another day, and I guarantee you'll be pointing to a different person, even if the differences may be very small.

Why is it we believe so fervently in an identity which is ephemeral?

What happens to the character when the TV is off?

When you are in a deep sleep, there is no sense of who you are, what you do for a living, your relationships or your challenges.

The sense of "I am" and everything that comes with it is only switched on when you wake up.

It's like a character who only comes to life when the TV is on - our character is in abeyance until we awaken from the deep sleep.

Just like the images which fleetingly appear on the TV screen, so the nature of our character is intermittent, transient.

The images on the screen are a projection of the TV.

Our character is a moment to moment projection in Consciousness.

We would never believe the projected images to be the TV.

Why does it make sense to believe we are the character, and not Consciousness?

Let's go fly a kite

All too often, we believe our emotions to be like kites, buffeted by the winds of fortune.

We forget that in order to have an impact, emotions need an anchor point, and that anchor point is the self - the ideas and stories we have about who we are.

Without the reference point of yourself, who is there to experience emotion?

To like or dislike someone or something, that someone or something has to have meaning.

It has to have a relationship to an "I".

It has to appear separate from an "I".

The truth is, we are not the kite.

We are not the boy desperately trying to control the kite.

We are not the winds buffeting the kite.

We are not the sky which is the stage for the airborne action, and we are not the ground on which the boy stands.

We are the space in which these things appear.

What we experience are momentary creations of Thought, which take form with varying degrees of vividness and impact within Consciousness, before fading back into their formless foundation.

Knowing your true nature will not exempt you from the winds of fortune; nor will it suck the joy or the meaning out of life.

For as long as you are human, you will have a sense of self to one degree or another.

An anchor point.

And that's no bad thing.

In coming to see your character for what it is, you are less limited by your perceived boundaries, more open to the vastness and potential; able to enjoy the twists and turns, the highs and lows of the journey, without believing that any of it is a reflection on who you really are.

Tear down the wall!

"All in all, it's just another
Brick in the wall."

The famed Pink Floyd album *The Wall* tells the tale of the fictional rock star Pink, whose traumatic experiences cause him to build a wall around himself, cutting him off from family, friends and even his own true self, in the name of avoiding pain.

While his story of excess is extreme, it is one we all share to one degree or another.

From an early age, every experience we have is a brick.

Many are meaningless and instantly discarded, but those that have meaning - the victories and defeats, the first flushes of love and the painful breakups - are used to create the walls of our identity.

By building this identity, we tell the world who we think we are – I'm Phil, I'm a husband, a father, a son, a brother, a corporate worker bee and a sports lover.

We devote lots of time to embellishing the façade we present, seeking to add ever more impressive bricks, trying to build a really large wall.

The more bricks that are added to this wall, the more the true you is obscured.

But no matter how many bricks are added, the true you remains unaffected.

In the classic album track "*The Trial*", the judge orders:

"Tear down the wall!"

The judge knows that doing this will expose Pink to his peers. It plays on Pink's greatest fear - that without the wall he will be left vulnerable to more pain.

What really happens when anyone's wall is demolished?

What is revealed is that which was there at birth: the ever-present backdrop to every moment of our lives - the sense of being, the aware space in which all bricks of experience appear, and of which all are made.

Are we vulnerable to pain and trauma? Yes. But we are also vulnerable to joy, love, pleasure and all manner of wonderful experiences.

Trauma and pain are not the absence of the wall, they are bricks in the wall.

The wall is a temporary structure.

It does not define us.

Our birth right – the sense of being – is without boundary, infinitely creative and offers infinite possibilities.

Dare.

To.

Tear.

Down.

The.

Wall!

Who is the imposter?

Many people suffer from what is known as "Imposter Syndrome."

Impostor syndrome has the individual doubting their accomplishments and plagued by the nagging fear they will be exposed as a "fraud".

Despite evidence of their abilities, they are convinced they are undeserving of success and attribute what they get to luck.

They feel they are deceiving others into thinking they are more intelligent, more capable than they really are.

The truth is, not one of us is who we believe ourselves to be, and in that realization lies liberation.

We all accumulate a collection of beliefs about ourselves, which over time we model into an identity the way a potter models clay into the form of a vase.

There is, however, less inertia about humans than vases.

In claiming any identity – including that of being an imposter - we are pretending we have a fixed form.

But our form is never fixed.

Our body shape changes.

We gain weight, we lose weight.

We grow hair, we lose hair.

Our eyesight and hearing changes over time.

No two breaths are ever the same, although they may feel similar.

The perceptions we have change:

Do you still see yourself as the same person you were as a five year old?

Is your relationship to the world still the same?

Are your relationships with other people the same as they were when you were five?

Is your circle of relationships the same?

Do the people who know you all see you the same way?

Look back over your life and you will see how much is always changing.

Now, think back to those times when you had little or no sense of identity – when you were lost in a stunning sunset, or in a dreamless sleep.

Where was your identity then?

If that identity was truly fixed, wouldn't it always be with you, 24/7?

Would there ever be a time when it wasn't there?

Even if you have no sense of identity, you still exist.

There is still a sense of being.

Can you recall a time in your life when there was no sense of being?

That sense of being was there when you were little, when you grew, when you learned to walk, talk, read and write, when you went through school and when you went out into the big wide world of adulthood.

It is what enables you to read this.

It is what enables you to consider yourself a success, or a fraud.

It is that from which identities are made.

Call it being, mind, consciousness, awareness, selfless presence, infinitely creative energy - use whatever words make sense.

It is who you are before identification happens.

Just as the vase is a limitation of the clay, so your identity is a limitation of who you truly are.

To know the truth of the vase, you have to look past the form it takes to the clay from which it is made.

To know the truth of who you are, you must look beyond your ideas of who you believe yourself to be and look toward the underlying sense of being.

An imposter is a person who pretends to be someone other than who they really are.

So, stop pretending to be who you are not.

Stop pretending to be an imposter.

Just be.

Am I living in a box?

There are not many people who would choose to live in a box.

Why then are so many people attached to their sense of identity?

Why do people suffer and feel bereft because they have lost their identity?

Isn't a highly developed sense of identity the ultimate box, hemming us in on all sides, tightly defining our limits?

Why would we want to feel so constrained, when our true self is so much more?

To those who feel they gain comfort from a highly developed sense of identity I would ask,

"Where does that identity reside?"

"What is that identity made of?"

"Can you show me your identity?"

For anything to be true, it has to be permanent and unchanging.

In other words, your true identity has to be an unchangeable constant.

If it changes, if it can come and go, it cannot be who you truly are.

Your identity cannot be your body, because that changes from day to day.

It cannot be your family, your possessions or circumstances, because those change as well.

Your name was an appendage that was added sometime after your birth.

There was a time when you had no name.

Isn't it true that your sense of identity is based on stories about yourself that you have bought into?

The tellers of these stories might be your parents, your friends, those you don't get on with, those who may not even know you personally but have an opinion of you.

Very likely, the biggest teller of stories about you is you.

In buying into these stories, you have made yourself a box, stepped inside it and said,

"This is the limit of who I am."

What's to be done?

See the box for what it is, a thought, with as much permanence as breath on a mirror.

Look beyond the box, look to the stars. Look beyond the stars.

What is it that enables all experience, yet is prior to all experience?

Isn't there a simple awareness?

You have the capacity to experience your fingernails.

You can also experience distant galaxies.

Without awareness, you couldn't experience them.

Can you find a boundary to awareness?

Can you find anywhere that awareness is not?

Awareness is without boundary – it is everywhere and ever present in experience.

Since it is what enables all experience, awareness is primary, transcending all limitation that thought appears to impose.

Since there are no limits to awareness, there are no limits to experience.

So, let go of any limiting ideas about who you are.

Dare to discover your vastness.

Who owns the house?

I was listening to a talk given by my friend Dr. Ken Manning when he said something which hit me like a ton of bricks:

"I just know that things are a lot better when Ken is not around."

What I heard was that when Ken's ego takes a backseat, things seem to work a lot better.

Isn't that true for us all?

When Phil is convinced he has a personal stake in things, he becomes very attached to how things go and the way they turn out. He is concerned the outcome will reflect on who he is, how he is perceived and how his future happiness may be affected. He feels the need to interfere, because he believes that without his help, things will obviously go wrong.

The evidence however, suggests things work perfectly well without his interference.

He's had years of thousands of actions being co-ordinated for him while he was blissfully unaware of them.

He's pretty rubbish at telling the future. He's not put a single bookmaker out of business.

And he doesn't always know best – as his beautiful wife will confirm.

But occasionally, when Phil's not around, it leaves in charge the intelligence which ensures he neither misses his mouth with a fork, nor puts his foot in his mouth when speaking with his wife.

And things work out pretty well.

So well in fact, that one day while Phil was not around I did try changing the locks.

But he found a way back in.

That's ok though, because I know Phil is just a house guest.

Not the owner.

The web of self

It seems we spend lots of time battling problems.

It's interesting that some things we consider to be the end of the world may not cause others to even blink.

Situations that are stressful to some may leave us completely unperturbed.

Why is this?

Problems are only problems because of how they relate to our sense of self.

The more we think about "me" and relate to things in terms of how they affect "me", the worse it seems to get.

This sense of self is like a cobweb in a living room.

The larger and denser the web, the more flies it catches.

The more developed our sense of self, the more problems we find.

What if I suggested that our sense of self has as much permanence as that cobweb?

You might argue that one a bit.

But what is a sense of self made of?

Is your idea of who you are the same as it was when you were born?

How does it compare to when you were twelve, or when you were twenty five?

The sense of self is an accumulation of experiences.

It changes all the time, as new experiences revise or replace old ones.

Once the sense of self is seen for what it is – an ever-changing myriad of experiences – its solidity diminishes.

It shrinks.

As it does, our relationship to problems changes.

Problems need an owner.

They need a sense of self to be caught in.

No sense of self, no problem.

A load of Pollocks

When we are born, we are but a pencil point on the vast page of life.

As we get older, that pencil point gets bigger and bigger as we grow, gain knowledge and enlarge our sense of self.

Increasingly, this sense of self covers ever more of the page. The pencil point becomes a Jackson Pollock like creation splurging outward towards the very edges of the page.

We stretch ourselves, because we want to grow, to become more, to fill the page.

In a sense, we want to be the page, because the page is everything.

And then - just maybe - we begin to question who we are.

As we do, we come to see more and more of the basis for this sense of self.

We come to see that it is constructed of experiences, ideas, relationships.

We come to see it is made of thoughts with no objective or factual existence.

And the more we see that, the more the sense of self begins to diminish.

It retracts.

If we look long enough, the sense of self may revert back to being a pencil point.

It may even disappear, leaving naught but the blank page.

At which point, we disappear into the page we dreamt of being.

We become the page which is everything.

The ironic thing is, we always were the page, because the self we believe ourselves to be emerged from that page.

The page was always the unseen background without which the pencil point would have nothing to appear on.

We always were the blank, empty page of unlimited potential. The pencil points, the expansions and contractions of that, merely momentary expressions on that page.

The sense of self is a mischievous scamp and imposes boundaries which lead us to believe we are limited.

But that's a delusion.

The delusion of self.

What are you carrying?

There's a fabled story about two Buddhist monks wandering along a country path, who encounter a stranded woman unable to get past a huge puddle in her way.

Without thinking, one of the monks picks her up, puts her on his back, wades through the puddle and places her safe and dry on the other side.

The two monks continue on their way. The monk who had watched his compatriot's action is troubled and after a time can no longer hold his peace, and asks:

"Brother, you know our order expressly forbids touching women in any way. Why did you do that?"

The other monk looks back at him with kindness and replies,

"I put that woman down long ago. Why are you still carrying her?"

This lovely tale tells of the perils of becoming limited by your identity, by thoughts about who you are, who other people are, what the "rules" mean and the all too human habit of projecting a consequence onto an action, as though the future is cast in stone.

One monk was completely consumed by who he thought he was, and what his order might do to him if they found out what happened.

The other was in the moment, unlimited by any fixed thoughts about who he was, the order he belonged to and their rules.

He simply saw another human being in need of help and acted.

He was selfless.

What is it to be selfless?

It is not to think of oneself.

In other words, a self is the creation of the thinking that one has about oneself.

Thinking is impermanent, and since what is true never changes, our thinking cannot be true.

Since the self is a creation of thinking, that can't be true either.

So, if we can't be a self, what we must be is self-less.

To be truly selfless is not only about being a better person.

It is to recognize who you truly are.

Whose portrait is it?

It is said in Buddhism that enlightenment is the end of suffering.

What causes suffering?

From very early on in our lives, we start to paint portraits.

These can be portraits of ourselves, of other people, pets, or the world we see around us.

We tend to compare any portrait we paint to the one we have of the way things should be.

Comparison creates suffering.

Suffering kicks in when something differs from how we want it to be.

It could be that you have a job, but it's not the one you want.

You might want your co-workers to see things as you do, but they don't.

Maybe your partner or children are not perfect.

Maybe you are distressed by the images of poverty and conflict that you see on the news.

You may go in search of people or situations that are closer to your ideal.

For a time, you may even succeed.

But we tend to forget that other people and situations - as well as our own ideals - are changing from moment to moment.

The relationship between where we are at and where we want to be is always in flux.

Eventually, we may decide to pursue enlightenment.

But can we truly enlighten ourselves?

No, because the ideas we have about ourselves are not the truth but a portrait - and a portrait can't be enlightened.

Enlightenment lies in realizing we are not the portrait, but the artist holding the brush.

Enlightenment lies in knowing that the artist is not an individual, but the Consciousness from which all portraits emerge.

What is the source of experience?

Managing thoughts and feelings because we don't like them is the equivalent of the ocean trying to quell the waves, or the sky trying to rid itself of the dark clouds obscuring the sun.

In doing so, we forget our true nature.

We must look past what is created, and towards that which is doing the creating.

What is before suffering?

What is before feelings?

What is before words?

What is before thinking?

What is it that enables us to be aware of these things?

The ocean does not try to quell the waves.

The sky does not try to rid itself of the clouds.

Let the words come and go.

The thoughts come and go.

The feelings come and go.

The suffering come and go.

They are not who you are.

You are not limited to being the waves, you are the ocean.

You are not limited to being the clouds, you are the sky.

You are not limited to your experience, you are the Consciousness within which this arises.

Does this experience define you?

When thoughts create feelings of upset, it is because those thoughts seem to relate poorly to the image we have of ourselves and how we think the world should be.

They can seem to be a commentary on the state of our life.

They are taken personally.

They are identified with.

And this causes pain and suffering.

When beset by such thoughts, you can try asking a simple question -

"Are these thoughts, who I am?"

What this question really asks is -

Do the thoughts that are being experienced in this moment define who I am?

Are these thoughts the sum total of who I am?

Inquiring in this way challenges the solidity of ideas which, in the moment, appear to place limits on our worldview, on who we are and what we are capable of.

There are innumerable variants of this question, to address whatever seems to be the source of unease.

"Are these feelings, who I am?"

"Are these people, who I am?"

"Are these circumstances, who I am?"

Look closely, and you will notice that experience of any thing - thoughts, feelings, circumstances, people - is momentary.

Transitory.

Fleeting.

Here one moment, gone the next, like a cobweb in a living room, a cool breeze in the air, or images on a movie screen.

What is true, is unchanging. That which changes, cannot be true.

If any thing is transitory, can it really be the truth of who you are?

If the transitory thing cannot truly be you, what difference does knowing that make to the experience?

If these things are not who you are, then who are you, really?

Consider for a moment, the cobweb in the living room, the breeze in the air, the images on the movie screen.

Isn't there a permanent background, an unchanging stage on which these things appear?

The living room in which the cobweb appears.

The air in which the breeze appears.

The movie screen in which the images appear.

What is the permanent backdrop to all experience?

Is Consciousness, who I am?

Who knows?

When you were newly born, you had no knowledge of language, no words for anything in your field of experience.

You had no idea that the wiggly things you felt moving about were arms and legs.

You didn't know they belonged to you.

You had no notion that the woman looking at you adoringly was mummy - you didn't know what a woman or a mummy was.

You had no clue that the green smocked beings buzzing around were doctors and nurses, or what the machines going "ping!" could be.

After a few days there was a prolonged spell of motion, which you had no inkling was a car taking you home.

Life was a continual stream of wordless perceptions and sensations, one after another.

Some felt good, some not so good.

Sometimes you gurgled and other times you cried.

But there were no stories attached, because these only come with language.

With language, comes distinction.

With language, comes comparison.

With language, comes separation.

The canvas of perception seems to tear into an increasing number of fragments.

The world appears to divide into a subject and a myriad of objects.

Into a "me" and a "not me".

Language moulds every experience we ever have.

Pay attention to your immediate surroundings and remove the words.

I'm not saying this is easy – the relationship between words and anything in our field of experience tends to be very strong. Consider any object, and multiple words will immediately leap to mind.

But, to the extent that you can, experience without words.

When there are no words, what happens to ideas about -

How the world should be?

How things should go?

What other people should do?

What happens to relationships?

To separation?

To conflict?

What happens to your own self-image?

If there is inherent truth in anything, it will remain after the words are gone.

What you really are, is before language.

When you were born, you had no words.

Therefore, you are before words.

So, what are you before words?

You might say nothing.

But in order for you to know that, doesn't there have to be an awareness of that?

WHAT IS PRIOR TO THOUGHT?

Who is waving?

Believing that experience has an existence separate from Consciousness is like the ocean envying the waves which caress the beach.

A drop and the ocean

Why fear the loss of individuality?

Does a drop of water fear falling back into the ocean?

In doing so, the drop of water becomes the ocean once more.

In losing our individuality, we recognize ourselves as the infinite Consciousness that we have always been.

Can't see the wood for the trees

In playing the game of life, Consciousness distracts itself from itself and yet – while it may appear otherwise – the essence of our experience is never anything other than Consciousness.

Why do we lose sight of that?

For the same reason that we get so preoccupied with what's going on in Central Park that we forget it's all happening in the United States of America.

Obscured by clouds

Just as the sun still lights our world when obscured by clouds, so our true nature provides the stage on which life plays out, even though it may be hidden by the scenery and the action.

What comes first?

There is a legend that the day and night were disputing which was the more important.

They could not agree, so went to the sun as an arbiter.

The sun did not recognize either.

The sun is before day and night.

It illuminates the earth, and by doing so creates day and night.

The sun is the primary creative element.

Day and night are secondary effects.

Our sense of self and our image of the world tend to consume our waking hours.

But, just like day and night, they are secondary effects.

To know your true nature, look to the primary creative
source –

What is it that knows this sense of self and the images of
the world which dance before us?

The phases of the moon

Our true nature no more changes than the moon has phases.

Just as the moon appears as different shapes in the night sky throughout the month, so our nature seems to be shaped by the thinking we experience.

In reality, the moon is always a sphere. It only appears otherwise because of changes in its position relative to the earth and sun.

Despite what thinking may have us believe, our true nature remains that of being the space in which this thinking appears.

Prêt-à-porter

We wear clothes, but few of us would dream of saying,

"I am the clothes."

The sense of being, that subtle energy which is the backdrop to every experience, similarly wears the body.

But for some reason, it does not seem silly to say,

"I am the body."

And yet, it really is no different.

The diamond mine

Much time and many words have been devoted to the idea of self-improvement.

It is often seen as a key ingredient to a successful life.

What is this self we want to improve made of?

From the beliefs, experiences and stories that we have taken to be our own.

Why do we pursue self-improvement?

So that we may project a good image of ourselves.

Image is defined as a representation or a general impression. It is also defined as a simile or a metaphor.

In other words, an image is an approximation of reality. It is not reality.

Your self-image is a distortion of who you truly are.

Who you truly are is the infinitely creative energy which enables the experiencing of life.

Why go jewellery shopping, when you live in a diamond mine?

Candid camera

Consciousness is so integral to our everyday experience that we struggle to see that there would be no experience without it.

Why do we overlook something so obvious?

Because Consciousness is like a camera.

A camera records our lives and the things we experience.

But how often does a camera take a picture of itself?

Hidden in plain sight

"I am that by which I know "I am.""

Eight short words from the Indian sage Nisargadatta Maharaj, which simply describe our true nature.

The bedrock of existence.

Hidden in plain sight and taken so much for granted we are oblivious to it in the same way that a goldfish is oblivious to the water in its bowl.

Without it we cannot experience thought, create identities, form relationships or tell stories.

Without it, we can't experience life.

What is this bedrock of existence?

It's a sense of being.

A sense of aliveness.

It's Consciousness, the infinite fishbowl in which we all swim, the support system for all life that is, was, and ever could be.

Who is the author?

Imagine you are an author.

You have had a long, distinguished career and written countless books which have sold millions of copies and garnered you worldwide renown.

You sit in an easy chair in your office, surrounded by your impressive library.

You have written every word. Every character, plot, beginning and ending, has been crafted by you.

One day, you are so immersed in the writing that you become completely convinced you are one of the characters.

You suffer and exalt as you are subjected to every plot twist and turn.

You worry about what will happen, about whether the story is a long or a short one, about how things will turn out in the end.

You are trapped on the page being written in that moment, experiencing whatever is happening.

You rail against fate. You wonder why you are happy one moment, downcast the next.

You struggle to improve your lot.

Sometimes it works, sometimes it doesn't.

You wonder why you have so little control.

You desperately want to be the author of your own fate.

At some point, it occurs to you to ask the question,

"Who is the author?"

And as you reflect on this, you are magically restored to the easy chair.

You always were the author.

Just not as the character.

Where to look?

An archaeologist goes to a dig site where untold treasures are known to be.

But once there, the archaeologist decides to go digging someplace else for these things.

This is exactly what we do when we go looking for ourselves.

We spend thousands on books and courses.

We go to far flung parts of the world like India, Tibet and China.

We seek out gurus.

We may even climb mountains.

All in the pursuit of who we truly are.

Why does it make sense that who we truly are isn't right here with us, right now?

How can who we truly are be anywhere else?

How can who we truly are be anyone else?

You are always here - you are the one watching the drama.

The trouble is we forget that and leap into the drama, believing we are the situations and circumstances playing out in front of our eyes.

We forget that what plays out in front of our eyes is a projection of Thought.

We forget that who we are looking for is before thinking.

We forget that who we are looking for is right here, doing the looking.

We are not experience; we are that which experiences.

The archaeologist must dig deep, then look beyond the rubble to find their prize.

Next time you are caught up in the rubble of thought and don't like what's happening, ask yourself,

"What lies beneath this thinking?"

You may make the greatest find of your life.

Serenity now!

There's a famous episode of the American sitcom *Seinfeld* where the normally volatile George announces he has found a new sense of calm through use of the mantra, "serenity now".

Whenever he feels his temper rising, he repeats the mantra and is calmed.

But as the episode progresses and George faces more and more challenges, his renditions of "serenity now" have an increasingly louder, fraught edge to them, until finally he explodes.

The episode is a slick, funny take on the all too human tendency to believe that desirable states like peace are things to be acquired.

Emotions, both the ones we enjoy and those we don't, are expressions of our natural state.

Watch a baby for any length of time and you will observe a being who swings from delight to distraught and back again in a matter of moments.

In babies, such strong emotions are common, but fleeting. They don't last long enough to become states.

The reason for this is very simple. Emotions pass through quickly because babies do not identify with them. They do not have a concept of who they are yet, so they can't identify with anything else, either.

But as adults, we have well defined ideas about who we are, what we like and dislike, what's right and wrong.

Because of that, we tend to think about every experience in terms of how it relates to us.

Based on that, we decide whether the experience is a good or a bad thing.

Emotional states can be prolonged, but they don't define who we truly are.

They are products of the beliefs held in that moment, beliefs which change too much to be true.

Our true state is before any identities, situations or accompanying emotions.

Who or what is it that remains, when your identity is nowhere to be found?

Find that state and you just might find serenity, now.

A muted thought

The mute button on a TV is an incredibly useful thing.

Wouldn't it be nice to have a mute button for our thoughts?

For those times we are overwhelmed?

For when we are consumed by worry and stress?

Thoughts are continually passing by in Consciousness like stories in a news broadcast.

Why is it sometimes we are completely gripped by those thoughts and other times we don't even notice them?

Because sometimes it seems those thoughts say something about you or your life, and other times it doesn't.

Often it appears that without the capacity to think things through, our lives would grind to a halt.

But is that true?

Just for a moment, pretend you do have a mute button for thought.

What would that be like?

How would it affect your ability to emote, judge, label and relate?

Cast your mind back to a time when the volume of your thinking was turned down.

Wasn't there still a sense of aliveness?

Doesn't that sense form a backdrop to your every moment?

What happens when you focus on what is experiencing, rather than what is experienced?

"Triomphing" over the mind

All of us suffer from busy minds at one time or another.

Busy minds cause stress, anxiety, overwhelm and all sorts of feelings that we would rather avoid.

So prevalent can these seem to be, we can become convinced these feelings are our natural state.

But that's like believing the natural state of the Arc de Triomphe in Paris is the traffic circling around it during the day.

Stand at the Arc de Triomphe at dawn, and there will be considerably less traffic.

The traffic is an activity within the Arc de Triomphe.

The busy mind is an activity within our natural state.

The amounts of traffic, the busy-ness of minds – these change.

Our natural state is not changeable.

What is our natural state?

What is it that enables us to know how much traffic there is at the Arc?

What is that enables us to know whether our mind is busy, or calm?

Isn't there an observing presence?

Can you experience anything prior to an observing presence?

Was there ever a time in experience when this observing presence was absent?

Is there anything more basic to our nature than an observing presence?

The greatest gift

Some talk about the importance of staying in the present.

The truth is, there is nowhere else you can be.

If you are ruminating over an argument you had with your partner a week ago, or dreaming of the sun-drenched holiday you are looking forward to, when are those things being experienced?

In the present moment.

There is only the present moment.

Ramana Maharshi said:

"Let what comes come; let what goes go. Find out what remains."

The great sage was talking about who we truly are, and about how that which comes and goes cannot be true, because it is transient.

What is that comes and goes?

Any experience you can ever have. Whether it be thoughts, feelings, circumstances or situations, they are always changing, even when it feels otherwise.

Look hard enough, and there will always be differences.

Maybe obvious, maybe imperceptible.

The happiest of people have times when they don't feel so good.

Those suffering from overwhelm or tragedy have moments of respite, even if those moments are so brief they go unnoticed.

That which comes and goes cannot be true.

Only that which is constant is true.

That which we truly are never goes anywhere. It is always here.

What is it that is there before, during and after all thoughts, feelings and experiences?

Presence.

Presence is always there, and all we can know.

Presence, the basis of who we are and common to us all.

Common to us all, and infinite.

One presence, experiencing a never-ending present, via the billions of gifts it creates.

Taking the Mickey

What if I were to tell you that off-camera, Mickey Mouse really hated Goofy, that he compulsively worried about the stock price of the Disney Company, and once had a bitter contract dispute with Walt, which nearly saw him leave to go work with Bugs Bunny and Elmer Fudd?

Several responses might spring to mind.

But if you were in a kindly state, you would point out that Mickey Mouse is a cartoon character.

Mickey is not creating; he is being created, by the animators at Disney.

The stories we associate with Mickey are those like *Steamboat Willie* and *Fantasia*. But for any of those stories to come to life, there first has to be an animating presence.

Now, what if I were to suggest that we humans are like Mickey?

Your responses to that one might be a little less kind:

"Are you freaking kidding me!?! I have financial worries, bad relationships, my job might stink, but I can go find another one. How can you compare me to a cartoon?"

Well, is it absolutely true that you - the person - are the primary creative agent in life?

If the animating presence – the life force – were removed from your character, what could you experience?

Which came first in your experience – the name you are known by, your character and life history, or the animating presence?

For anything to be experienced, there first has to be an animating presence.

This animating presence is primary. Being primary, it is our true nature.

It is what creates the human experience.

As humans, we are like Mickey in that we are not animating - we are being animated.

The human avatar

The movie *Avatar* tells the story of the human exploration of a planet named Pandora.

The humans go there in search of energy sources to replace those being rapidly depleted on Earth. Unfortunately, the atmosphere on Pandora which supports the indigenous Na'vi tribe is poisonous to humans. To explore the planet, scientists use Na'vi human hybrids called avatars, which are remotely operated by genetically matched humans.

The avatars have no life of their own - they are lifeless until inhabited.

Every thought, feeling, intent, word and action is determined by their operators.

The avatars are being lived.

While thinking often has us believing otherwise, Consciousness is not a creation of human beings.

Human beings are a creation of Consciousness.

Which came first, the idea of who you are, or the capability to have that idea?

If humans are the controlling power, why is there so much in life that we find uncontrollable?

That there are so many uncontrollables in life, suggests that a greater power is in charge.

That human beings are an expression of that power.

That human beings do not experience but are being experienced.

That what is experiencing is the power which creates that experience.

That human beings are avatars of Consciousness.

Dream character

Recognizing yourself as Consciousness is like waking from a dream.

A dream can be so convincing that you experience the same emotions and physical reactions as you would encountering that situation in the waking world.

You can be dreaming you are a superhero, saving the world by foiling your arch-nemesis's dastardly schemes in a variety of death-defying ways.

Being a superhero, you are revered, an object of gratitude, awe and adulation.

You may feel limited by your identity, though. Being the defender of the world might be a privilege, an honour, but also a burden, and you long for the day you can tell the one you love who you really are.

Despite your powers, you may still feel a very small part of a very large world.

But no matter how compelling and realistic this dream, everything about the story, the setting, and yourself, are all happenings within the dream.

The superhero is not having the experiences. The dreamer is having the experiences in the guise of the superhero.

When we are in the dream we so believe that we, the superhero, saved the world! But upon awakening, we realize that not just the superhero, but the entire dreamscape, was a projection.

We recognize ourselves as the dreamer, and not the dreamed.

As we wake up to the dream of life, we realize that our persona and the world we inhabit are thoughts, appearances within that which is aware of those things.

Anything that is experienced is an appearance within the Consciousness which is our true nature – a nature which cannot be limited by any identity that we believe to be ours.

Nothing ever lasts forever

I was listening to the famed Tears for Fears hit, *Everybody Wants to Rule the World*, when I was struck by the line,

"Nothing ever lasts forever."

No thing – people, buildings, circumstances, situations – lasts forever.

All things come and go.

As much as people don't want change, it happens every moment of every day.

Jobs and relationships come and go.

Buildings are raised, and buildings are razed.

Every cell in your body has been replaced numerous times.

In clinging to the wish that the world would not change, we are clinging to a world which does not exist.

Aligning ourselves with a world that does not exist can result in disappointment and pain.

Why not be open to change?

To acknowledge how the world really is?

How would getting comfortable with the idea of constant change alter your experience?

We suffer because we identify with that which changes.

But that which changes, does not define what we are.

What we truly are, is that which gives rise to the world and everything in it.

That which, because it gives rise to all things, is before all things, and is therefore, no thing.

It is that which is before any concept, such as time.

You, me, our relationships, houses, families, work and recreation are all appearances within it.

It remains while everything else comes and goes.

Everything we could ever experience is made of it.

We are not limited to human bodies.

We are only limited by the boundaries of the creative energy of which all existence is made.

Boundaries which no one has ever found.

"Nothing ever lasts forever."

We are no thing.

We are beyond forever.

Show me the true London!

Visitors to London are often left in awe by its rich history and the monuments which give the city its identity - The Houses of Parliament, Buckingham Palace, St. Paul's Cathedral, The London Eye, The Shard, to name but a few.

When we think of the word London an image of the city springs to mind.

But the character of the city has changed over time.

The London which emerged from The Blitz during the Second World War was significantly different to the London before it. The same can be said of the city that arose from the ashes of The Great Fire of 1666.

There was a time before any buildings were on the land that is now London.

A time before the settlement and the name of it even existed.

There would have been rough, unkempt land, and a growing tributary around which London would one day arise.

Most people don't think about that, being too fascinated by the sights and sounds surrounding them.

In everyday life, we are so busy figuring how best to tackle whatever is in front of us, that we rarely stop to ask how the character of our lives has changed over time, or to wonder what our lives were originally built on.

We fixate on thoughts, feelings, situations, the roles we play, and act as though these are cast in stone.

We may claim these things as our character, our identity, and tend not to notice the moment to moment changes which are forever happening.

Like London, we change over time.

Like London, there is a foundation on which we are built.

There is something that exists before we have a name, before we know any of the things - parents, partners, children, jobs, hobbies and so on - which we come to think of as monuments to our identity.

What is it that has always been present throughout your life, through which all the stories, situations and people that helped build your identity were experienced?

Isn't there a simple awareness?

An awareness which, while untainted by any identity or story, is also the space in which identities and stories are born and grow?

London could not exist without the landscape on which it is built.

We could not exist, without the awareness which is the foundation of every experience we ever have.

You might be cloudy, but you are still the sky

Imagine a clear, cloudless sky.

It is a beautiful day.

The sun shines brightly, bathing everything in its golden glow.

Then clouds begin to form - light, fluffy and innocent at first, but becoming increasingly dark and menacing, spreading across more and more of the sky, until barely any blue can be seen.

Then, the storms breaks and the rain lashes down, soaking everything in its path. The wind whips up, buffeting the trees and any pedestrians unfortunate enough to be out in it.

Is this storm the true nature of the sky?

No. The clouds, rain and wind are all temporary forms which take shape within the sky.

Thirty minutes later, the clouds have dispersed, the wind has dropped, and the puddles have dried. The sun again shines brightly in an otherwise blue panorama.

Whatever the weather, it leaves no permanent mark on the sky.

Our true nature is like that of the sky.

We are the clear space of Consciousness, within which thoughts form like clouds.

Thoughts can be so compelling we can believe they are capable of permanently altering our true nature.

We might try to manage those thoughts – but that's like trying to manage the weather.

We do not control the coming and going of thoughts any more than we control the coming and going of the rain.

Thoughts appear in Consciousness whether we want them to or not.

It might appear as though thoughts can batter and beat us, but thoughts never leave a permanent mark on Consciousness.

They are temporary experiences within that which we truly are.

A greater intelligence

How often do you use a laptop without connecting to the internet?

Do you restrict yourself to the hardware and software in that laptop when searching for answers?

The internet has transformed the value of the computer. Where once we worked with limited information, we now have access to a seemingly infinite amount of it.

Knowledge that used to require hours of research and study is now at our fingertips in seconds.

Human beings are like laptops.

We have an intellect, which is an incredibly useful tool - but it is limited.

It does not always give us the answers we are wanting, and often we cudgel our brains in a desperate attempt to force them.

Yet how frequently do answers come to us when we are not even thinking about them, like when we are showering, or out for a walk?

When we are not placing all our eggs in the basket of intellect, it allows a greater intelligence to shine through.

A greater intelligence we cannot be disconnected from, because it is what we are made from.

We have access to so much more than we think, because we are so much more than we think.

We are not limited to the intellect, because we are the ultimate internet known as Universal Consciousness.

Which knows all that can be known, is never off-line, is always available with the answers, and knows when they are needed.

Look within what, exactly?

Groucho Marx famously said,

"Outside of a dog, a book is man's best friend. Inside of a dog, it's too dark to read."

A lot of confusion is caused by the term "look within".

What does that mean?

Where is that?

Where should I look, exactly?

The main culprit in the confusion is the belief that you are limited to being a person in a body - that's a small space to look within, and it's pretty dark in there!

But consider this –

How do we experience?

Where are the limits of experience?

How do we experience things beyond those limits?

Syd Banks once said:

"There is nothing outside which can help you, there is nothing outside which can hurt you, because there is no outside."

The raw material from which experience is composed is our ability to be aware and to think.

Anything we experience occurs within Consciousness and is shaped by Thought – and since that includes everything from within the body to the distant stars millions of light years away, those are pretty big limits!

Our experience of the whole universe happens within us.

You could say, the whole universe is within us.

Or, that we are the universe.

When you are told to "look within", you are being advised to investigate the very building blocks of experience.

Consciousness and Thought.

It all happens within there.

There is no experience without.

The zone

In sports there is much talk about the zone and how to get into it.

The zone is characterised in many ways.

An effortless state, where time slows down.

Knowing how the play is going to unfold before it happens.

Anticipating gaps in the defence which magically open, right on cue.

A state of no thought.

An out of body experience.

Look at any of the great teams during a performance that is hailed as perfection, and it is as though the individuals merge into the team's unwavering and magnificent pursuit of its goal.

The movements seem part of a divine, preordained choreography.

I'm thinking Phil Jackson's Chicago Bulls, Pep Guardiola's Barcelona.

Such teams - at least at times - exude a state of excellence that finds full expression when individuals are absorbed in something greater than themselves.

You might say that in those moments of perfection they exhibit selfless presence.

Selfless presence is another name for the zone.

The zone is a state that is whispered about in awe-struck tones.

It is seen as somewhat mythical, attained by the blessed, gifted few, and even then, only fleetingly.

What if - rather than something to attain - it is something we already are?

Something that is only veiled from view when we are apparently lost in thoughts about ourselves and what we are doing?

What is a self, other than the stories, thoughts and experiences that are accumulated and identified with?

If the self was who we truly are, it would always be with us.

But there are moments in life when we lose all sense of self:

Moments of transcendent performance.

Watching an amazing sunset.

Being left speechless by the awesome grandeur and silence of the Grand Canyon at dawn.

When we are in deep sleep, or under anaesthesia.

Since there are moments in life when there is no sense of self, the self cannot be who we are.

Which makes us selfless.

Yet in those selfless moments, something remains.

That which remains is what we are.

That which remains is a sense of presence.

A selfless presence.

Another name for selfless presence is the zone.

Not a mythical state, not something to be strived for, or a state to get into, but what we are, right here, right now, and always.

Who is in control?

Understanding how the human experience works does not exempt you from being human.

It doesn't eliminate thoughts and feelings.

As human beings, we have things to do, others to take care of, questions to answer and choices to make.

From a physical point of view, you have a body which can be damaged, and it makes sense to take care of that body as best as you can.

Standing in front of a speeding bus yelling,

"You can't hurt me, you are just a projection of Consciousness!"

is unlikely to protect you from harm.

Telling your inert husband,

"You're a figment of my imagination, you lazy git!"

will not cause him to disappear, or make you feel any better. He'll be slumped on the couch until the football is done, and even when he does disappear, the beer cans will still be there as evidence.

You will have situations which will mean a lot to you, and you are going to want them to play out in a certain way.

But understanding how the human experience works, enables you to live in a lighter way.

It's the difference between playing a World Cup Final on a games console and playing in a real one.

You don't have ultimate control of the joystick in life.

Life is going to play out the way it's going to play out.

You can do your very best to try and influence the outcome, but you know that it's not down to you as an individual.

You just do what makes sense in the moment, see what happens, and go from there.

Whatever does happen, is no reflection on who you truly are.

It's not personal.

One ocean

Some time ago I asked my then eleven year old daughter the question,

"How many oceans are there in the world, sweetheart?"

She pondered this for a moment and then answered,

"One, daddy."

When I asked her why she gave that answer rather than the traditional one of five, her response was simple:

"Well, where are the joins?"

The oceans of the world are one body of water. We simply use labels like the Atlantic Ocean and the Pacific Ocean to make it easier to pinpoint which part of the single body of water we are talking about.

By applying these labels, we create a separation which does not physically exist.

Many people are confused when it is asserted that we are all oneness, or one being.

It appears to most everyone that there is an immense amount of separation out there – billions of objects, animate and inanimate, billions of creatures, human and otherwise.

But what are all objects and creatures made of?

How are all these objects and creatures experienced?

For anything to be experienced, there must be a life force, an animating presence, which can be sometimes known as Mind; a capacity for awareness or Consciousness; and a power which creates objects in awareness, which we sometimes call Thought.

Remove any of these three capacities and there is no experience of anything.

Experience is made of these capacities in the same way that waves are made of ocean.

Because they are fundamental to experience, these capacities are principles.

You could refer to these three principles as a sense of being.

Where are the boundaries to the sense of being?

Can you locate the sense of being?

You might argue that the sense of being is in the body.

But is it really limited to the confines of the body or does it extend beyond the body to encompass everything in your experience?

For example, if the sense of being does not extend to the stars in the night sky, how can you experience those?

You can't – your experience of those stars is within the sense of being.

There are no boundaries to the sense of being.

It is infinite.

The meaning of "infinite" has been defined as limitless or endless in space, extent, or size; impossible to measure or calculate.

This infinite sense of being is something we all have.

How many infinite things can exist?

There can only be one.

Otherwise, it would imply that one infinite thing was larger than other infinite things - which would then, by definition, no longer be infinite.

If this sense of being is infinite – and we all have it - that means we are all the same, infinite sense of being.

Or one being.

Or oneness.

What do we have in common?

Recently I was intrigued by a social media post entitled, "Racism for dummies".

Consisting of two photographs, the first showed three eggs - one pink, one brown and one white.

The second showed the eggs cracked open - they were indistinguishable.

We live in a world of so much conflict - country versus country, politicians versus the people, arguments about race, religion, gender, sexual orientation, physical attributes - the list is endless.

Conflict means difference.

The more we look for differences, the more we find.

The more differences we find, the more separation and alienation we encounter.

How different might the world be if instead of differences, we focused on what we have in common?

We all have our hopes, fears, likes and dislikes.

We all have our causes.

We all - even those who seem to be the most misguided - do what makes sense in the moment, otherwise we wouldn't be doing it.

No matter who you are, where you come from or what your story might be, your every experience is a creation of thought.

Thoughts are experienced within Consciousness.

Even your experience of yourself is a thought creation within Consciousness.

Consciousness was present before there was any concept of you or your parents.

Consciousness is aware of you now.

It is the aware presence that has been a constant in your life.

There is nothing which can be experienced outside of it.

The limits of Consciousness have never been found - it is infinite.

Being infinite, it encompasses us all.

No matter what the colour of our shell, we are all appearances in one Consciousness.

There is no other.

Conflict of any description needs at least two parties.

What would it mean for conflict if we were to know ourselves as one?

One being, many reflections

Imagine being alone in a hall of mirrors.

There are twelve mirrors in the room, arranged so that as you stand, you are in the middle of them.

As you glance at each, you see yourself reflected.

In each mirror, your reflection is slightly different.

But while there are twelve distinct reflections of you, there remains only one you.

Because of the angles they are at, the mirrors reflect and appear to "perceive" one another. They can "interact".

Yet the only true observer of these mirrors is you at the centre.

Any movement perceived in these mirrors is coming from you. The reflections have no volition of their own.

Now imagine one being, alone in an infinitely vast hall of mirrors.

The mirrors in the hall number over seven billion.

Each mirror shows different aspects of the being at its centre.

Between the mirrors there are still differing degrees of "perceiving" and "interaction", depending on their position in relation to one another.

But there remains only one true source of these reflections.

That source is also the observer of the reflections and the actor responsible for any movement in the seven billion plus mirrors.

The being in the middle of the mirrors is Consciousness.

The mirrors are the human race.

It appears that we are humans having a conscious experience, but in fact, we are Consciousness having many, many human experiences.

Different expressions, same essence

You might wonder,

"How can we be one, when our lives and experiences are all so different?"

It's a bit like whirlpools in the ocean.

The whirlpools may be in different places within the ocean. They may be of different sizes and oscillating at different speeds.

But occasionally in their movement, they touch one another. Intersect. Merge.

In such moments, they are in the same space, their experience localised and shared.

But whatever form they take and wherever they are, the whirlpools remain made of water, within the same ocean.

Similarly, our human experience may sometimes feel individualised and sometimes shared.

Sometimes we share a similar space and other times seem to be separated by continents.

Yet we remain made of and exist within a single Consciousness.

What remains when the last layer falls away?

Discovering who you truly are is like peeling an onion.

Layer after layer disappears and just as we joyfully believe we are about to see what is at the core, the last layer falls away and we realize that there isn't one.

That what's left, is absolutely nothing.

Or, that there is no longer anything separating us from the experience of being absolutely everything.

The energy behind life

The life force which animates us is similar to the electricity that illuminates the lamp.

When the lamp is switched off, we do not lament that the electricity which powered it is lost forever - we know that it still exists.

Plug in a different lamp, and the electricity will illuminate that one.

So too with the life force - when a person dies, the life force which animated the person still exists, it just no longer animates that body.

The force which gave that body life existed prior to the birth of that body and will exist beyond its passing.

That force is the same one which surrounds us, infuses us, creates ourselves and the world we experience.

It was never born, and it will never die.

At the end of the day, what is the essence of the person, really?

The body of the person, their physical and mental attributes, or the animating presence which brings the person to life?

The work of art within

When Michelangelo was asked how he created his famous sculpture of *David*, he reputedly remarked that he "chipped away anything that was not *David*."

Apocryphal or not, such a comment is a recognition that the raw materials needed for such a masterpiece were already there.

Nothing additional was needed, *David* was already latent within the marble.

He just needed to be freed.

What would it mean for our lives if we were open to the possibility that we already have everything we need?

That, rather than adding, we simply need to subtract whatever is not useful?

I'm not even keen on the word "subtract".

Really, it is to know what we already are.

We spring from the formless creative energy that is the bedrock of all life, an energy which is infinite, without boundaries.

Nothing can exist outside of it, because it is everything.

Trying to add things to that is impossible.

How can you add to something that is already infinite?

You can't.

What's more, you don't need to.

Being made of that energy, you are everything you could ever need.

You are the marble, and *David* is already there.

Unlimited knowledge

Recently a planet was discovered that has baffled scientists, because its existence contradicts accepted theory about how planets are formed.

The planet – which is snappily named GJ 3512 B – formed around a star which apparently is too small to have provided the material for a planet of such magnitude.

In responding to the find, scientists expressed their excitement, because they have wondered for many years whether such large planets could form around relatively small stars.

This story highlights the brilliance of scientists.

But their brilliance is not limited to how often they get it right.

Their brilliance is due in no small part to how often they are wrong.

And how willing they are to be wrong.

If you never get it wrong, what is there to learn?

How often though, we pride ourselves on what we know.

So much so that we can get quite upset when things run contrary to what we believe in.

If you always get it right, it means that everything is known.

And clearly, there is not a single person on the planet who does not have something to learn.

It's just that people are uncomfortable with the unknown.

But the reality is we live in the unknown every second of every day.

We may believe that we know ourselves and other people and how the future will play out, but we don't.

We might think we know what is for the best, but we don't.

Not really.

As people, we cannot understand the bigger picture in which we live.

A human being is a limitation of that bigger picture, an edge of a portrait that cannot possibly appreciate the whole masterpiece.

Human beings do not know.

Human beings do not know because they are themselves expressions of a greater power.

In the same way that a lamp is an expression of electricity, human beings are expressions of Consciousness.

Everything that is experienced appears within Consciousness and is made of Consciousness.

There is nothing than can be experienced outside of it.

Anything that can appear in Consciousness is known.

Because it encompasses anything that could ever be experienced, Consciousness is knowing.

Because Consciousness is our true nature, knowing is what we are.

But as human beings we are a limitation of that knowing, which is why there will always be things which will remain unknown to us.

And that's ok.

It's what makes us curious, it's what inspires us to explore distant galaxies in an endeavour to understand more about our universe.

It's what makes us human.

Is it possible to go against the Ineffable Plan?

Good Omens tells an alternate version of the Armageddon story.

In this wonderful tale by Terry Pratchett and Neil Gaiman, the Anti-Christ is put on earth by the Devil but is given to the wrong family. He grows up a nice, well-adjusted kid, and rather than bringing about the end of the world, saves it.

The agents of Heaven and Hell know that when the boy turns eleven, his evil powers will find full expression, the Four Horsemen of the Apocalypse will ride and the great celestial war will begin.

Both sides see this as inevitable and are preparing themselves. For victory, of course.

Aziraphale, a conscientious and warm-hearted angel who is delightfully naïve to the corporate politics both upstairs and down, fights to avert Armageddon. Over the millennia, he has come to love humans and doesn't want them to be destroyed.

His efforts are much to the chagrin of his fellow angels, who advise him not to do anything that is against God's Ineffable Plan.

But here's the thing – "ineffable" means too great or extreme to be described in words; incomprehensible, indescribable, unknowable.

So how is it possible to know whether what you are doing is in line with The Ineffable Plan?

Surely, if everything is part of God's Ineffable Plan, it is not possible to do anything that is contrary to it?

Surely every action must be part of it?

In everyday life we like to pretend that we know what will happen. That we can predict the reaction to every action, that we control the outcome.

If that were true, everything would go to plan.

But it doesn't.

And this is the difference. Our individual plans are knowable, but life is ineffable.

We are hoping to impose knowable plans on an unknowable life.

It is this striving - to make life the way we want it - that causes suffering.

As individuals, we are very effable.

The good news is that we are not limited to being the individuals we believe ourselves to be.

For what is an individual, other than a collection of ideas and experiences, a collection of thoughts?

Thoughts are not truths, they are momentary impressions, here one moment and gone the next.

All thoughts, all experiences - including those of being an individual - take place within a Consciousness which is the creator, the experiencer and the experience.

Who we truly are is too great or extreme to be described in words; incomprehensible, indescribable, unknowable.

Who we truly are, is ineffable.

The Supreme Being

According to the religions of the world, the Supreme Being is omniscient, omnipotent, and omnipresent.

All knowing, all powerful and everywhere.

In other words, there is nothing the Supreme Being does not know, nothing they cannot do and nowhere they cannot be.

That being the case, is there any chance the Supreme Being can not be you?

EPILOGUE

People often remark on how laid back I appear.

And much of the time these days, that's true.

I'm generally pretty relaxed about how things turn out. I understand the person I believe myself to be and my ideas about life are all thought creations, including this idea that I can know the future. I can't possibly know how things will turn out, and the outcome is influenced by far too many other things and people to be within my control.

I can only do the best I can, based on what I know in the moment, and see what happens.

I tend not to identify with situations, and know that how they turn out has no reflection on who I truly am.

When I do identify with what's going on, it's because I've temporarily bought into the idea that Phil is more than a creation of Thought. That he will be diminished if things don't go his way.

We all have our moments, and many of mine happen on the golf course.

I love golf - and it also drives me nuts.

While intellectually I understand that Phil the golfer is no less a thought creation than anything else in life, on some level, I don't really believe it.

It's not an embodied understanding.

What do I mean by an embodied understanding?

Talk to any smoker and they are unlikely to try to convince you that smoking is good for your health.

They still smoke anyway.

They will quit when the understanding that smoking is not healthy becomes embodied - they not only intellectually understand it, but naturally live it too.

With golf and I, it still seems that Phil the golfer is important on some level.

Phil the golfer was created forty years ago.

He has hit lots of good shots and achieved a fair level of proficiency. He won tournaments, represented his county team in his youth, held a single figure handicap for a few decades and broke par on a number of occasions.

You can hear the pride in that little list, can't you? That's Phil the happy golfer talking. He identifies with those things as being a true representation of what he is all about.

But he has also hit awful shots and had terrible rounds where he couldn't hit a cow's backside with a banjo. On those days, Phil makes veiled threats never to play again.

He doesn't like those days and does his best to forget about them.

Phil the golfer has good days and bad days.

Days that prove he is capable of greatness, dross and everything in between.

Why would he choose to associate with some shots, some days, and disassociate from others?

Because some shots and days feel good, and other ones feel terrible.

He prefers the good days and the feelings they bring.

What makes something good or bad?

The words good and bad are nothing more than comparative yardsticks, which move according to who is doing the assessment, and when they are doing it.

At the golf club where Phil grew up, he played with three excellent golfers who became his benchmarks. To compete with them, he had to get better. When he played well, he was worthy of their company. When he played poorly, he was a pariah.

It never occurred to him that everything is dependent on your viewpoint in the moment.

At some clubs, he may not have sniffed the top ten best golfers.

At others, he may have been far and away number one.

His good would be to Tiger Woods, pathetic.

His bad might be dreamed of by some golfers who have never scored less than a hundred.

What is golf, anyway?

A game made up by shepherds to while away the time, because there are moments when sheep just aren't that exciting.

The game, what it means and the measurements of good and bad are all made up.

The only person who really cares about how Phil the golfer plays is Phil the golfer.

If someone goes looking for Phil the golfer, they won't find him.

Sure, they may find golf shoes, clubs, balls and a bag.

They can even find a person dressed in a golf shirt and slacks, answering to Phil's name, using that golfing equipment.

They can watch that person hit shots, and from those shots, and their knowledge of golf, frame an opinion of who Phil the golfer is.

But the opinion won't be true.

Phil, and Phil the golfer, did not show up at the same time as the body which became known as Phil.

A human baby was born, the character known as Phil showed up sometime later and Phil the golfer later still - he always was tardy in getting to the tee.

Phil the golfer is just a story, just as Phil in any guise is a story, woven from the thousands of stories told about him since birth.

Any experience that anyone can ever have is a story.

Stories which are being embellished, changed and sometimes binned, from one moment to the next.

Stories which are woven from thoughts.

Any experience one can ever have – including the experience of the individual they believe themselves to be – is a creation of Thought.

The thoughts which create our world and experiences are not truths, but momentary, limited perspectives.

That which is true is unchanging, and that which changes cannot be true.

That which we truly are is unchanging.

Take away the stories, and what remains is that which we truly are.

What remains is that in which all experience appears and is what all experience is made of – call it Consciousness, awareness, selfless presence, or a myriad of other suitable synonyms.

The word is not that to which it points.

What you truly are, is beyond the power of words to describe.

The human thing can be pretty compelling.

And that's ok.

I like being human.

It's a great game.

ACKNOWLEDGMENTS

I'm so lucky and grateful to have been guided by some wonderful people.

Garret Kramer set me on this path, and the skilful sharing of others such as Sydney Banks, Dr. Aaron Turner, Jamie Smart, Michael Neill, George and Linda Pransky, Barb Patterson, Elsie Spittle, Jan and Chip Chipman, Dr. Keith Blevens, Valda Monroe, Sandy Krot, Dr. Ken Manning and Robin Charbit has been instrumental in deepening my understanding.

To the following dear friends:

Dr. Amy Johnson, for giving me continual encouragement and an audience to develop my ideas with.

Elissa Clash, Michelle Furne, Chika Izuakor, Amanda Jones, Neil Root, Alan Smithies, Grant Telfer and Phil White for kindly offered feedback and encouragement on rough drafts.

The fabulous dad and daughter combo, Mark and Amy Carter, for their fabulous cover artwork.

Bonnie Jarvis, for her help in turning that fabulous artwork into a superb book cover.

Cris Hay, for being my de facto editor and constant sounding board.

Jonny Bowden, for his kind and excellent foreword, encouragement and numerous conversations which have taken me ever deeper in this understanding.

Fred Davis, un-teacher extraordinaire, for blowing my mind and showing me unequivocally what I am not. You totally changed my perspective, for the better.

To my beloved, departed mother and brother, for giving me the best possible start in life, with never ending encouragement, support and love. You are with me always. My sadness in your not being here is tempered by the belief that you are together again, bickering away in front of the telly like some Celestial Gogglebox, and having a fine old time.

And to my wonderful family who put up with me going on about this way more than I should – I could not be luckier or more blessed in you sharing my life. To my lovely outlaws, you have always made me feel as one of your own. To my beautiful and amazing Debbie, Lulu and Lexie (and our Yorkshire Terrier ball of fluff Clemmie) – no words can describe how much I love you all.

And to you, dear reader. If even one of the metaphors in these pages has given you pause for thought, this book has done its job.

I wish you joy in this fabulous and mind-boggling journey called life, even during those bits that you wish were a bit different.

There is so much to see, do and experience – what a privilege.

My love and best wishes go with you, always.

ABOUT THE AUTHOR

Phil Hughes is just over fifty but likes to think he is not speeding. He lives in Sunningdale in England with his wife and two daughters who get even more beautiful with every passing day, which should not be possible but apparently is. Sadly, the cat who shared their lives for fifteen wonderful years has now passed to kitty heaven. The roost is now ruled by a Yorkshire Terrier who believes she is a wolf.

This is his second published work, after a previous book of psychological metaphors entitled, *It's All in the Mind, You Know!* published in 2018.

Please feel free to reach out if you would like to discuss anything about this book!

I can be contacted at:

Email: philanthonyhughes@gmail.com

Facebook: phil.hughes.3785

Printed in Great Britain
by Amazon